I STAND CONVICTED

I STAND CONVICTED

◆

THE TRUE STORY
of an
Innocent Man
Who Was Guilty As Sin

R. L. "Duke" Tirschel

Ryan Larosa

God Bless You

Duke Tirschel

Isaiah 40:31

iUniverse, Inc.

New York Lincoln Shanghai

I STAND CONVICTED
THE TRUE STORY of an Innocent Man Who Was Guilty As Sin

iUniverse books may be ordered through booksellers or by contacting:

iUniverse
2021 Pine Lake Road, Suite 100
Lincoln, NE 68512
www.iuniverse.com
1-800-Authors (1-800-288-4677)

ISBN-13: 978-0-595-34574-8 (pbk)
ISBN-13: 978-0-595-67129-8 (cloth)
ISBN-13: 978-0-595-79321-1 (ebk)
ISBN-10: 0-595-34574-3 (pbk)
ISBN-10: 0-595-67129-2 (cloth)
ISBN-10: 0-595-79321-5 (ebk)

Printed in the United States of America

I dedicate this book to Joan, the mother of the three children I left behind. Her strength and courage took over when I lost mine.

Because of her, three wonderful children became three wonderful adults, and this world is better off because of it.

Contents

Preface

In the book, "I Stand Convicted", I describe the bizarre behavior I thought would make me a man. Because, that's what I wanted, I wanted to be a man. I wanted to be a man so much, that I was blinded by my very desire to be a man. It wasn't that I was just lazy or that I didn't *want* to grow up. I didn't grow up, because I didn't *know how* to grow up.

People don't *choose* to make the wrong decision just because they *want* the worst that life has to offer them. Many of the wrong choices we make are made simply because we don't know what the right ones are.

By definition, you don't see a consequence, until it's upon you.

My heart goes out to those who fell to, "If I knew better I would have done better". Because, when I fell, I found the worst in me, and the worst in the people around me.

But I saw something else that I chose to hold on to; I saw greatness; I saw warmth, and compassion. I saw extraordinary kindness. And I saw brilliance, where no one would ever expect to find it. I saw *that the best* that was in the worst of us was as grand as anyone's best could ever be.

I have faith in the decency of the down trod. I see hope, as an anticipated expectation, for the mistake riddled souls who know there is something magnificent in them, yet to be found. I believe in them because I believe in me, and I *am* one of them.

I want to turn back from this place, that I've reached in life, and yell, "Watch out, it's a trap, we took a wrong turn. Go back. Before it's too late, go back."

But, we know better, don't we? It's always too late to go back.

We'll never make right, what we've done wrong, nothing can be *undone*. But the beauty of it all, and here's the trick, ***nothing needs to be undone***. You don't have to go back, to start over, and it's never too late to begin again.

Your starting line is right where you are, right now.

When I grew up late in life, I was old enough to stand back and understand what I was watching when I saw the boy in me become a man. That's why I believe in *us* old kids, and why I know we can still grow up, no matter how old we get.

One can't say it's a trip worth waiting for, because in a perfect world, it's much better to grow up when you're "supposed" to; but still, if you are ever to say that you truly lived; you will have to, *have grown up.*

Throw away the labels that hide from you the role to which you were made to rise, and become the man that God created you to be.

That's *how*…to grow up.

Acknowledgments

To everyone who has ever been good to me and to everyone who has ever been bad to me; and each of you will know which ones you are.

I thank you for what you taught me.

Introduction

My life at twelve years old was pretty simple.

But, I still remember my first glimpse of manhood. It came to me when I saw a boy standing on the corner waiting for the light to change.

I don't know how he did it.

I was amazed that he stood there absolutely oblivious to the epiphany taking place. I never saw him before that day, and I never saw him since. But, in that one brief encounter, fifty-two years ago, he exposed to me a part of life's puzzle for which I was the missing piece. And so, it was on that day, I began searching for the exact place in which I might fit.

I didn't know the difference between a good or bad childhood, or that any other kid's life was any different than mine.

There were a lot of things I didn't know, at that age.

But, I still sensed in many of those things I didn't know, the existence of critical information, placed there specifically for me at the precise time I was supposed to see it.

This boy looked to be my same height and roughly my same build. But, at the same time, he appeared to be so totally different than me that I couldn't think of him as just another boy. What I saw in him was something to grow into, something that you're supposed to be ready for after you have finished being a boy.

A cocoon can work magic and change a furry little caterpillar into a butterfly. But. the metamorphosis, to which I was a witness to that morning, wasn't that of a butterfly, but that of a man. I was the caterpillar, and that boy I saw had obviously emerged from some metamorphosis, to become a man.

What is that magical process that turns a boy into a man?

How do I get from what I am to what that other boy appeared to be?

How do I be that?

For the first time in my life it occurred to me that a man was not just a taller, older boy. A man had spirit, all together different, from that of a boy.

I decided right then; that was what I wanted to be…a man.

I stood a few feet behind him, watched him, and took a mental note of every detail that was different about this boy. That was difficult to do in such a short time, but I did see one very noticeable difference. He wore the tight blue Levis that had the little red tag on the back pocket, and I wore baggy Jeans.

I was certain that I found the answer to the question of becoming a man.

My eyes were opened that day, to something I didn't understand, and my pursuit of the mystery of manhood began by wearing a pair of Levis. I also judged my friends by that little red tag on their back pocket.

Men only hang out with other men.

And so, I actually looked; literally, physically looked for that red tag on the back pocket, before I accepted any of my friends as a fellow man.

That began my belief that various stages of manhood could be found in the different labels to which a man would fight to own.

After the red Levis tag, I went after my manhood again and again, but each time, I chose a different label: being a clown in school, some woman's opinion of me, how smart I was, how much money I made, or how many people I could hurt and who was scared of me.

I quickly lost sight of the rise to become a man, and began to take pleasure in the labels that would tell others that I *was* a man.

Some of the people in my world did read in those labels, what I wanted others to think about me. But I never found the label that told *me,* I was the man I wanted to be.

Could it be…that, for which I was looking might not be found in a label?

I searched for my manhood everywhere "out there", and never once did I consider the fact that I might already possess what I'm looking for, inside here; inside of me.

But, there's always a catch…even if I did already possess it, and even if it was somewhere inside of me, I would still have to find it.

1

Arm in arm, two off-duty strippers from last night's party crowd staggered out the back door of the Crystal Palace and into the blinding morning light. Surprised that the day had already started, they groaned in unison, "Hell no" and abruptly turned and went back inside.

My car was one of the dozen or so cars still sitting at the front door of the club but I was out here in the empty parking lot. Together, the upper and lower lots were about the size of a football field, and I wandered out and stood alone in the middle of the upper one and waited for San Ji.

I recently took to wearing a silly red bandana that barely fit my head. My hair was too long, and it curled out at the sides and ran down the back of my neck. I gathered up as much hair as I could fit into a handful, put a rubber band around it, and called it a ponytail. I wore black combat fatigues that tied at the ankles, an inch or two above my dirty sneakers.

The chill in the early morning air gave me another good reason to be wearing my full-length long black leather coat. My teeth grit, my nose flared, and my eyes sunk back into a scowl. I placed my hand beneath my long coat, and tightened my grip on the Mossberg shotgun. San Ji was turning into the parking lot and aiming his Mercedes in my direction.

San Ji had become the largest dealer of amphetamine "speed" in Atlanta.

My reputation was built on the street's rendition of executive protection and collections. It wasn't all that much, but it gave me a major part in the drama being played out on the south side of Atlanta.

Big frog-little pond sort of thing.

His side you get high…my side you get hurt. We were both at the top of our game at what we did. Now, we were having a heads up *friendly* talk. I didn't know what he had in mind but I know I had something I needed to get off my chest.

Neither of us was high, drunk, in the middle of anything going down, or just passing through as we ran from the law. We had the time to talk it out.

San Ji's face slowly appeared as the dark tinted window lowered, "Hey Bro…whatzup." He peered over the Christian Dior sunglasses worn low on his thin nose. He reached a soft, well-manicured hand out the window, and I grabbed it coldly with my free hand, "San Ji…hey man, what's up!"

San Ji removed his glasses, took his time putting them in their case, and then placing the case into his glove compartment before getting out of the car. With arms held high and wide he cocked his head to one side and stepped forward to hug me, "My friend…my friend, it's so good to see you." He smelled of Calvin Klein and silk and money. I wondered how aware he was that I was so much different than him.

Surely my unshaven, ruddy face and matted hair, my dirty hands, and the smell of four straight nights with no sleep said all there was to say about the mess my life was at the time. The contrast I was to San Ji would have embarrassed me a few months ago, but now I accepted what I had become. I couldn't sleep, nor did I want to, not until I could see San Ji and ask him one simple question.

But before I could ask it San Ji said, "Oh did you hear…Ronnie got popped last night?"

"Yeah…that was stupid. Why'd he take his girl along…that was stupid? It was because of her you know? The deal wouldn't have gone down like that…without her there."

"You gotta keep the women out of your business, Duke. You can't let them get the best of you, man…once they set-up shop in your head; you won't be able to think straight."

I nodded my head in agreement but I was thinking of something else, or at least I thought I was. I felt uncomfortable by his talk of Ronnie's woman with what I had on my mind. I wondered if San Ji had a purpose for bringing up Ronnie's deal going bad.

He must know the reason I wanted to see him and maybe that's the reason it took so long for him to show. Now, I didn't know how to say what it was I wanted to say, so after an uncomfortable silence I just came out with it, "So how's Kiwi doing?"

"You tell me. She's *your* girl."

"If she's my girl why is she sleeping with you?"

San Ji smiled as he slowly walked over to the open door of his car and leaned over and reached for something above the dash. I slid the Mossberg's sling off my shoulder as I started to pull it out from under my coat and level it towards San Ji.

Life slowed down to a crawl and like the voice on a film running in slow motion I heard the words that I was thinking...*do I really want to do this thing?*

An image appeared in my head of a bird, flying over Stewart Avenue, looking down on the Crystal Palace. He could see the two huge parking lots in front of a yellow and orange rectangular building. There are less than a dozen cars parked in front of the door leading into the club. Trees frame the building on the back and left side. On the other two sides are parking lots, one reaches up towards Stewart Avenue and behind a liquor store. The front parking lot runs to Connell Street that separates the Crystal Palace with the low-rent trailer park across the street. A black girl, with way too many pounds on her for the short tight skirt she's wearing, slithers up Connell Street. She motions to any car that passes her to come back...shop is still open.

The bird, like me, wonders if last night's business was that bad, or was she that determined to earn her way out of the trade. A spot in my heart is made soft for her, whatever the reason she's still at work, so early in the morning.

The bird circles back as something shiny caught his eye.

In the middle of the upper parking lot, standing by a black Mercedes, two men are talking. They appear to be friends but their voices don't show it, and the talk gets louder. The blonde haired dude is shouting. The other man reached into the car, and pulled out something shiny. When he turned back around with his out stretched hand, the blonde haired man stopped yelling. That caught the bird's eye, and except for one quick squawk, nothing else was heard but the flapping of wings heading for the trees.

When San Ji turned back towards me, the sun reflected off the metal of a shiny object that he held in his hand. When I saw it I smiled, I relaxed my hold on my Mossberg, and quickly flipped the flap of my coat closed.

"Do you remember this?" San Ji said.

It was a shiny medallion that had the sign of the Yin-Yang on it. It was on a strip of rawhide that was hanging on his rearview mirror when he drove up. On the rawhide there was also a pure crystal and a small feather with a painting on it. I now remembered where he got it.

He handed it to me and said, "You gave that to me."

It all came back, "Well I'll be..." I had forgotten all about it.

San Ji said softly, "Don't you remember...we were out one night...getting all messed up? I told you I was getting ready to go through bad times. You took this from around your neck and slipped it over my head and after telling me how much it meant to you, you said, 'Keep this with you always and no matter how tough things get for you, you'll find the strength to get through it'...remember that?"

I nodded that I did.

The night that I gave San Ji the necklace came back to me. I remembered how strong I felt that night. It must have been two months ago. I was strong then, I wasn't beat down or in the condition I was now. I was strong enough to give away what I thought protected me. It was always the memories that protected me. My protection had always been the memorabilia and artifacts that reminded me of something I searched for spiritually. And not sure whether I ever found it, I would hang my hopes on the artifacts and trinkets that helped remind me, of how scared and how brave, we can become all in the very same moment.

I saw that, whenever we're faced with annihilation, we stand and face it just because it's facing us. We seem to think it's our duty to give in to fate as it's screaming at us. It commands us to show respect, as though it takes dignity, to just stand there and take it.

But not me, don't put me up against the wall in front of a firing squad and think I'll just stand there. I'll come running; hands tied behind my back and blindfolded, I'll come running. I'll head butt you, I'll kick you, and I'll bite you…that is, if I can find you. And if I can't find you I'll run in the direction the bullets are coming from, so keep on shooting so I can find you; and when I come, I'll come running.

That was such a brave thought to think, but it sure is different when you're faced with the real thing. You see, I'm facing annihilation right now, but I'm not running. I'm being destroyed, but I'm not coming after anyone. I'm being hit and I don't even hear the shots being fired. San Ji is pulling the trigger of a weapon I didn't foresee, and as much as I try, I can't hate him for making me stand there and take it.

This is not the way it was supposed to be.

My martial art training left an image of a sign in my mind. I saw it once but I rarely did what it said. Now it's turned against me and I can't be the villain I want to be. The sign read: *"I destroy my enemies…by making them my friends"*.

San Ji is reminding me that we're friends, and he's destroying the enemy I thought we became. I can imagine now, why it took him four days to show up. He knew he would have to face me sooner or later.

I didn't think he'd come so heavily armed.

I'm being destroyed.

My mind wandered away from why I called this meeting. I looked at the necklace in my hand, and it was in that moment, that I became the old man that I was trying not to be. I thought fondly of times I've seen in the past, and again, I was reminded that it's been my memories that save me. I've always found a way, of latching them to something I can wear around my neck, or of tucking them in someplace safe, so I could visit them again. And in that way, I would have them whenever I needed to remember who I once was.

I've always been afraid to let them go.

I nodded again, "Oh yeah, now I do…I remember."

"Well Bro…it worked for me. I found a way out of the mess I was in."

I was curious since he didn't tell me, "What was the 'bad times' you were talking about anyway?"

"Oh that...I need to talk to you about that, but for now I just want you to know how much I appreciate you 'being there', for me, when I needed you."

I looked at San Ji and asked, "You giving this back? Are you finished with it?"

San Ji nodded.

I forgot all about my concern for Kiwi, and I was thrown back into the memories I once placed around San Ji's neck. There was a memory behind the Yin-Yang medallion, the crystal and the feather, and there was even a memory that came with the rawhide on which all these were placed.

I took a close look at the feather on the necklace, and I remembered it came from an Indian from Kansas. He said it was from "a spirit searching for his soul across the windy plains".

As I stood there with San Ji, I forgot everything. I forgot where I was, what I was doing, and I even forgot the reasons why I wanted to hate San Ji. But I remembered this necklace and what it once meant to me.

I wanted to talk about all the memories I held in my hand.

"See this feather...an Indian I met in the mid-west gave it to me."

Actually it was early one morning that he was sleeping in the back of a pick up truck in front of my motel room in Kansas. I was opening the door to my car when I heard the movement behind me and I jumped, "Whoa...Oh hi...I didn't see you."

"What time is it...are the stores open...do you think?" He hurried to get his shoes tied. As I watched him getting his things together I got the impression he overslept and he was late for something.

"I think they are...it's about a quarter..."

He interrupted me, "I have Crystals" and he pulled up a brown gym bag and opened it up. It was filled with rocks. "You just have to break these open and there will be a crystal inside."

Then he told me stories about the magic that crystals had done for his people. He followed me in and out of my room while I packed my van to leave. He stepped in front of me and said, "Here" and handed me a rock. "This is for you."

I thanked him and started bringing my heavy equipment out to the van.

When I went back into my room he had a half dozen charcoal drawings laid out on the bed, "Let me show you my drawings". There was a story behind each one and he gave me the drawing I liked the most, and along with it, a beautiful story about the drawing I chose to keep. I thanked him and he asked, "Do you think the store is open yet?"

"I think so." And then I told him I was about packed and ready to go.

"Let me show you feather earrings"…he gave me a feather earring with a painting on the feather, and again, a beautiful story that went it.

He showed me many wonderful things and I gave him my full attention because he seemed so eager to share this time with me. The art he showed me and the stories that came with them, were all beautiful, but none of them received anything from me but admiration and respect, sincere appreciation, and an overwhelming sense of awe.

All of that, and still, it just wasn't getting him what he wanted. So, finally he just gave up and said, "Let me cut to the chase…do you have five bucks you can spare so I can get a six-pack."

I did, and when I gave it to him he went in search of his soul and left me his beautiful feather.

I lifted the feather to the light for San Ji, "See that? That Indian I met in Kansas made the painting in that little space on the feather," I pointed, "right there. This feather is actually an earring."

"You know…?" San Ji paused a longer time than normal and as I waited for him to finish what he was about to say, an uncomfortable feeling grabbed me just as he ended his pause, and then he came out with it, "You know, I love Kiwi too."

I wish he hadn't said that…I felt uncomfortable him saying that…why did he have to go and say a thing like that?

Damn you San Ji, I thought…*damn you.*

I guess a bit of time passed while I stood with my mouth dropped open, holding the feather up to the light, because he continued speaking as if it were an effort to save me from what he thought I might be feeling. "Kiwi isn't *anyone's* girl…you know that. She doesn't *belong* to anyone. That's what she's trying to get across to you…not that she doesn't care for you, but that she doesn't belong to you."

Here's my friend...we've known each other for ten years and although we don't *have* the same things in life, we *like* the same things. It shouldn't be hard to believe we could want the same woman...but that's not good.

But neither could I find the bad in it.

Picking between a friend and a woman shouldn't be that hard in the crowd that we run in. My mind was racing...one hand holding a lovely Indian feather, the other tightening its grip on a short Mossberg shotgun.

I need to think this out.

I'm a college educated karate champion, and a bible toting fifty four year old man who dropped off the edge of reality to protect drug dealers, pimps, and whores. Twenty-nine year old San Ji was successful in the import export trade. He took the money he made from the import business and his karate school, and got a good start in the drug business. Now, he's one of the largest dealers of speed in Atlanta.

Kiwi? Well...let's face it...she's an eighteen-year old stripper, a drop-dead knockout beauty. She is physically, mentally, and spiritually endowed in a way that's beyond her years; I know a lot of women who would love to be more like her in every way, and she's just a kid.

She shocked me in the way she said goodbye one day. She said it in the kindest way, when she said, "I have nothing left to teach you...there's nothing left for me to do, but go."

Wow, she was only eighteen. I was fifty-four; now, what does that say about me?

So, should I accept this; her leaving me for San Ji? Do I choose the friend or do I choose the woman, or do I take the only choice I really have and wish them luck and leave them be?

San Ji's phone rings and he answers, "Ya...San Geee." He pivots so his back is to me. He takes a step away, nods and grunts a couple words in Korean as he gets in his car and then in English says, "Ok, I'll be right there."

Without looking back at me he says, "See you later Duke," and slams the door. I noticed for the first time that San Ji had kept his car's engine running while we were talking.

San Ji spins out on to Connell Street and passes a young black "working" girl with a skirt riding too high and too tight not to be noticed, and San Ji honks.

The girl waves, "Hey Geee…come back here. I got something for your skinny little…whoa baby."

Something flies out of the window and the "working girl" runs down the middle of the street, "Why Gee…you fool. You ain't got no sense at all". Out of breath, she stoops and scoops a little baggie off the ground, "Look here what I found" Her tired eyes turned quickly to catch one more glimpse of Ji's Mercedes before it reached the corner, at the end of the block. She raised her hand and waved and yelled out, "San Ji…you got a heart-a-gold".

A sudden disappointment hit me when his car disappeared around the corner. I felt small again. Mostly, because I knew I no longer played a role in Kiwi's life…not the role I wanted anyway.

But my biggest concern was that, this was not the way I thought our business should have gone. I was supposed to tell San Ji to stay away from Kiwi, and he should have said, "OK…I don't want to have any trouble with you. She's all yours."

Of course, she wasn't *all anybody's,* ever. But it was so nice to think she was.

"I won't be able to grab at that thought any more", I said out loud to myself and headed back in the direction of the front door of the club. It was a short walk back to my car but I learned a lot in the little time it took me to get there.

At first I was angry that San Ji and I never got around to finishing the business, the way I wanted it to go. But, as I walked down the stairs to the lower lot I began to smile. I realized that the important issue did get covered, and it was handled by San Ji in a way that showed respect for me.

The "bad times" he went through was even a larger issue that was placed on the table for a different time. That larger issue was one that San Ji introduced to me with the confidence that I could be trusted; and then left it, to be a reason that we could meet again.

Something good might come from that; we'll see.

Sometimes I think I'm smart…and sometimes not; but even when I believe I am, what I perceive, usually comes to me too late to use in a smart way.

I pulled out on to Connell Street and waved at the young black girl putting in the overtime. When I got to the end of the block I stomped the gas pedal to the floor, spun around the corner and laughed, "That's right San Ji…you got a heart of gold."

2

Another quick turn or two from Connell Street put me on I-75 south. It seemed a piece of my business had been accomplished, after four days of manipulative planning, calling and waiting. It produced a confusing result that satisfied me in a disturbing sort of way.

Everything I did these days seemed to confuse me more *after* I knew what was going on.

When something should have been clear to me, I was usually more confused instead. But in time, I discovered that the confusion wasn't about what was actually happening, I could figure things out pretty quick. It was about how I should feel, about what was happening, that confused me most of all.

Someone, I should be at odds with, just told me he was in love with my girl, and he told me as if to say there wasn't anything I could do about it. Then he just got in his car and drove away.

What's happening to me?

I thought I was the last guy on the planet that anyone would want to waltz up to and say, "I love your girl but since you and I are friends, don't sweat it."

My mind is not thinking right. This is crazy. Maybe I've just been up too long. I can't think straight. Maybe I should close my eyes awhile and think about this later on.

After four days of being awake I hear music no one else can hear. The music comes from a long distance off and sometimes I can hear voices singing, but I can't make out the words. It's not coming from any one direction. It's from all directions. Sometimes, I've been able to track it down and found that it was emanating from the buzz in a florescent light, or a finely tuned vibration that was inside the hum of a refrigerator, or an air conditioner. But most of the time, I discovered that the music I heard, after having been awake so long, came from the ringing in my ears.

It was when I was awake the longest that sleep was the hardest thing for me to do. The longer I was awake, after the first twenty-four hours of not sleeping, the less I wanted to sleep. Anytime I was up for three or four days I struggled violently against going to sleep. But, when it finally overtook me, I dropped to tremendous depths of sleep in the shortest period of time.

When I woke up, I would be so comfortable that I would just lie there absolutely still, and enjoy the feel of my body being held up by the gentle pressure of whatever was beneath me. The soreness in my body would slip away so slowly that I was able to actually notice, and enjoy the feeling of the soreness leaving, as it left.

After leaving the Palace I drove south, towards no place in particular, and thought of sleep like this, and my body went in search of it. I pulled into a parking lot in Riverdale and circled the strip mall of storefronts until I found a peaceful looking spot, with some good morning shade. I pulled into the shadow of a building of a Sign Shop that wouldn't be open for another hour or two.

After rolling the windows down a couple inches, I locked the doors, and lowered the back of the driver's seat. I laid back and began the long struggle of hallucinating, as I struggled to fall asleep.

Sleep finally grabbed at me, pulled me in, and when it was through with me, it woke me and when I opened my eyes I was totally rested. I was a new man with the same old problems, but at least I woke up to face my problems with a brain that no longer felt like jelly.

Go ahead, I thought, let Kiwi call *you...San Ji*. Let her tell *you* that she's in bed with Tony. Let her explain to *you* why she hasn't been coming home at night.

This thinking relieved me from feeling rejected.

That's right. Let her tell him all that crap, I don't have to hear it anymore. If I got upset about it, I was a "jealous little boy". If I didn't get upset she would just do more of the same until I *would* get upset and *then,* I'd be a "jealous little boy".

There was absolutely no way to win with Kiwi.

The sleep did me good and I didn't hurry to get up. I was comfortable there where I lay, in the cool shade enjoying these thoughts of Kiwi, and feeling more and more satisfied with San Ji being the one to deal with her from now on.

I never did get through to Kiwi.

But someone must have left a black mark on her somewhere, and in a very sad way, because she was listening to something in her head that put her too far 'out there'.

And that was a real shame, because this little woman was just a kid

San Ji was right; it was time for me to move on.

3

The party crowd, which included all the strippers, dealers, hookers, bouncers and such, from all the other clubs in Atlanta, that close at two in the morning, come to the Crystal Palace, stand in line to pay the cover charge, and get their hands stamped, so they can party on.

By six o'clock in the morning, there is a long line at the front door of the Crystal Palace. A couple bouncers work the parking lot and a few more are inside the club; but Daron, the head bouncer, sits at the chest high 'podium', collecting the cover at the front door, as the crowd files by. He's the one to say who can and cannot come into the club. I began teaching Daron in my karate classes when he was just a kid, and he eventually became one of my black belt instructors. And at one time, he ended up owning the first school I opened, which was in Forest Park.

Daron sits on a high stool with his muscular forearms draped across the podium in front of him. He has a large wad of fives and tens, in his left hand, with which he makes change. He'll place the twenties, fifties, and hundreds, in a drawer under the counter next to his 9mm, Smith and Wesson. A gold ring is on one hand, and two more are on his other hand. Around one wrist is a classy gold watch, and on the other wrist, a thick gold bracelet. One of the gold chains around his neck carries a huge gold piece that looks to be as much an investment as it is an ornament.

He stands six feet tall with broad shoulders and a broad smile. He's a good-looking kid with long flowing hair that hangs well below his shoulders. His girlfriend, Christy, is well aware of his appeal to the other women and so she stands guard on him, as diligently as he guards the club. Christy's a beautiful blonde who also wears a lot of gold, but not a lot of clothes. Her body's a chiseled piece of art and the way she displays her wares appeals to the men that come to the Palace.

She stands by Daron's side all night and gives a broad smile to the men and a cold one to the women. She's as sweet and as sexy as you'll ever see; but I guess the most beautiful part about her, is that she can really fight.

I never understood the relationship of her being so protective of *her* man since, for the years that she was *his* woman, Daron never hid the fact that when his work was done at the Palace, he always went home to his wife, Teresa, and their two kids.

I jumped the chain and walked around the people in line and waved to Daron on the way in.

Daron yelled over to me, "Mr. T. did you get your parking spot?" Smiling, he waited for me to answer.

"I sure did."

"I have that set up for you...from now on just come to the front...we'll save your parking place."

Since I rarely get to the Palace until the party's going good, finding a parking spot is next to impossible in the lower lot, and you have to be pretty lucky to even find one in the upper lot. But, right at the front door, along the front of the building there was a line of about 20 parking spaces that were filled with the first people to arrive. Off to one side were always three parking spaces that, when they were empty, had a huge barrel blocking anyone from parking there. Those spots were saved for Sid and two others that worked in the office. Sid owned the Crystal Palace and came to the club at 5am on Saturday and Sunday mornings. At 6am, he conducted the dance contest everyone knew as the "Stroking Contest". Dancers from all the clubs in town would compete, and it was the highlight of a "night" at the Palace.

When I drove up to the front, there was a fourth barrel blocking a space that Preston, one of the bouncers working the lot, was moving out of my way. He motioned to me, and waved me into that spot.

"Hey Duke...whatzup man."

I knew the guys would put extra barrels up, and sell the spots, so I took the spot and pulled out a roll out of my pocket. Preston raised both hands, with palms facing me, and gave a short quick push to the air, "No need man, this is for you. From now on this is *your* spot."

"Well, thanks man." I stood a little taller as I walked away and my chest was as swelled as my head. This is the way I liked to feel and the Palace let me feel it.

That's why I was there.

Two of the other bouncers saw me coming in and hurried over while Daron was asking me how I liked my new parking spot. They were big, muscular, and new at the Palace. I didn't know their names but they knew mine. The first guy raised his hand to shake in an arm wrestling position, with elbow bent, and hand held about face level. I had to raise my hand higher than he did to grab his huge hand. The fact that we both wore the same workout gloves, with the cut out fingers, told me a lot about him.

"Hey Duke, Daron told us all about you. Really glad to meet you man."

I didn't get his name.

The second guy stepped forward and we shook hands, "Yeah, me too, names Scott. You need anything at all, we're right here man."

Another bouncer was making his way over to us from the rear on my left. I saw him walking towards us out of the corner of my eye, but I didn't think anything of it. It was Buck, 6'8" and weighs in at 340 pounds. Since our first encounter he has always treated me with respect. I felt a gentle nudge on my elbow and when I turned in that direction, Buck was smiling at me, "For you Duke," he was holding out a cold bottle of Bud Light, "haven't seen you in awhile."

"Been around, sort of staying busy you know."

"Heard you been doing security work for Tommy at some of the rooms."

"Aw, we been talking about it. I still go to karate studios with my business." The truth was that I traveled around the country to karate studios doing my *photography* business but I didn't like to say the word *photography* around these guys.

It was my ego I guess. I just say, "I go to karate studios with my business."

I asked Buck, "I thought you were going to go to work over at the Gold Club."

Daron heard me and yelled over to us, "He wishes." Daron laughed, "The girls are too classy for him over there."

"Up yours, Daron," even in the low light I saw Bucks face turn red.

The rest of us laughed more quickly at Buck's rebuttal than we did at Daron's remark to Buck. We saw something in Buck that told us Daron's comment landed in the wrong place. I doubt that Daron knew how sore that spot was to Buck, when he said what he said. If Daron knew that Buck's girl broke up with him, when she started dancing at the Gold Club, I doubt that Daron would have made that remark. Buck turned down his shot to work at the Gold Club because of her.

Everyone standing there was on the same side, we were all friendly, but each one of us had our own personal sore spot. Usually when we go off at people, it's because some hidden sore spot, no one knows about, got rubbed wrong. Usually we explode without notice, and people just shake their heads and say, "Wow, what's wrong with him?" This time, we all stood around, we laughed, joked, and smoothed over any sore spots still exposed, as we carried on as macho fellows do. When the greeting time was over, Buck and Scott stepped aside for me to join the crowd, and I felt like quite "the man".

I needed that greeting at that time. I didn't know why, but they did.

About twenty feet to the left from where we stood, was a room with some foosball tables. Each table was taken and a few people were waiting their turn to play. Everyone who was waiting to play, faced the tables, and watched the games in progress.

But there was one couple not facing the tables.

They were facing me.

San Ji was leaning with his back against the cigarette machine, and facing the entrance, where I was standing. Kiwi was standing with her back leaning against San Ji, and his arms were wrapped around the front of her. That way they were both facing in the same direction, towards me.

Kiwi must have been waiting for our eyes to meet because when they did, she laid her head back on San Ji's chest and the corner of her mouth turned up into a very slight, but pronounced, "up-yours" type of smile.

I was amused more than hurt. I smiled back the same smile she was giving me, but I was more interested in the look that San Ji gave me. I once thought that when this moment arrived he would be more apprehensive, or maybe pretend he didn't see me, but he looked directly at me. Even from that distance, I could tell that he was trying to read *me*. Though his arms were wrapped around Kiwi, I saw an air of respect towards me. San Ji wasn't trying to send me any message.

His eyes looked directly into mine, and when he smiled, I saw a friend. He was a friend, 'feeling' for me, not someone trying to hurt me by taking something of mine away. The possessive stance he took was mixed with just the right amount of compassion, and that made me respect his right to have his turn with her.

I glanced quickly at the three bouncers and then at Daron. All of them were watching me, and then I knew, that's why I had my parking space, and that's why I was met at the door with a cold Bud-Light.

I wrinkled my nose, and made a face at Daron, as I threw one hand up in the air towards San Ji and Kiwi, and shrugged my shoulders.

Daron cocked his head and shrugged his shoulders as he raised both palms up to the air. He gave me his best *whatta-ya-gonna-do* sheepish grin.

I laughed and yelled over to the two of them, "Hey San Ji…whatzup?"

San Ji maintained his cool, lifted his hand slightly, and gave me a short nod with half a smile.

I saw the three bouncers relax and turn to walk away. I walked with them. I just really wanted to leave, but I couldn't. No way would I let San Ji and Kiwi take any more of me than they already had.

I thought it was so cool that my friends were there to watch my back. It wasn't to keep San Ji or any of his people from jumping me. They were watching for that chunk of my heart that was going to be ripped out when I saw Kiwi and San Ji together, and they were there just so that it wouldn't hit the floor.

They moved the huge barrel out of my way, presented me with my own parking space at the front door, they met me with a cold beer and a glad hand, and they stood with me in front of everyone and treated me like I was quite the man.

They weren't going to let Kiwi blindside me like that.

I doubt this day would be remembered by anyone else but me.

It was such a simple act that was meant to protect the inside part of me. No hardened eye would perceive the softness in the way these bouncers behaved that day. That's not the part of them they would want anyone to see anyway. But I saw it, and I remember.

I stayed a respectable time so that it wouldn't appear that Kiwi was running me off, but when it was time for me to go, I did.

"Gotta go," I said

"You heading out already?" Daron was checking ID's and taking in money and talked with me without taking his attention off the line of people in front of him.

I rapped him hard on the back of the shoulder and said, "I might be back in the morning."

4

I had no place in particular to go…I just wanted to go.

I'm an old war dog and I have no more tears to cry over women who decide I'm not what they want. But, I do admit that I still feel bad, when the glitter of who I was, no longer carries the weight of who I am.

I used to say, "Sooner or later, they all find me out."

I meant that women, sooner or later, see that I'm not all the man I'm cracked up to be. If they stay around long enough, they would see that I was enough man for any woman, but I was never enough man for me. And so, I always played the role of being more of a man than I was.

I took Connell Street, away from the lights of Stewart Avenue, into the darker side of no-place-to-go, and when I reached the corner I took the road leading towards a deserted industrial building. A sign that read, For Lease 100,000 Sq. Ft. hung down lopsided from the corner of the building. Some windows were busted out, weeds were growing through the cracked pavement of the parking lot, and the rusty chain link fence, that separated the parking lot from the freeway, was leaning halfway to the ground. The only light was from the headlights of the cars passing on the freeway.

I felt drained, mentally, physically and spiritually.

I pulled in and parked, and thought of the track my life was on, where it was going, and where it had been. My life must have jumped track at some point to be where it was now. It wasn't supposed to be this way for me. I couldn't remember where, or when, it turned south for me. I was trapped in the permanence of what I thought would be but a temporary peek at the "darker" side of life.

I leaned my seat back, rolled down the windows, and felt much like the cool breeze that was passing through. It too, had no place in particular to go.

I was comfortable enough to be willing to fall asleep, if that was where I was heading. But before I fell to anything at all, I closed my eyes and saw one bright and beautiful October day, that belonged to me, in a time that seemed so very long ago.

It was a Monday morning and I was leaving home to go to work. The early morning sun streaked through the pines in my back yard, and the backlit leaves gave off a blurry glow. On my way to the car I stopped, and I looked at the leaves in the back yard. They had turned orange and red and yellow and were in the process of falling to the ground. The naked limbs of the branches looked skinny, and revealed more of what was in the distance. I saw the winter coming on.

What I saw that morning was a beautiful sight and I vowed to write a poem about it some day. Then I got in my car and headed to the karate school I owned, a short distanced away.

I parked my car near the back door of my school and gave a quick short two fingered salute to the old wooden house with the gray stone chimney at the edge of my parking area opposite the rear of my studio.

There's a window on that side of the house and it's to that window that I directed a smile. Mr. Yancey's room was behind that window and neither his age nor his health allowed him much of anything other than to sit and look out that window facing across the lot to my studio.

I started waving in his direction when I first opened my school.

I could never see him sitting there but, in those days, I knew that if he wasn't asleep he would be sitting up in his bed looking out the window.

Mr. Yancey owned the property my karate studio was on, as well as the building next to me that had the Hair Salon and the one next to it that had the Dance school. He also owned the property on the other side of the driveway, where the store was and of course, he owned his house.

But even with all of that, all he really owned was that one small room in which he was confined, day and night. He also owned fifty years of memories of living in that house.

I made it a point to go visit him on days, other than just those days I paid my rent, and we would sit and talk. When I began my visits I didn't know what I would talk about, I just knew being there saying something, anything at all, might be a comfort to him. In time I realized it was the listening that was the greatest blessing of all, and I, the listener, was the one being blessed.

He told me all about the days that he and his wife moved into that house, when they were married, in 1941. He told me that when he and his wife moved in their home, the traffic on the four lanes of Forest Parkway was mostly horse and buggy, except for a few model T Fords that ran up and down what use to be a narrow dirt road.

I didn't talk much about my business, yet; he still knew I was struggling with it.

It used to surprise me that he knew most of my younger students, not by name, but by sight. He got a kick out of watching them going in and out of my school. He always had a comment about my students who entered the school from the back door, "How's that little red-headed boy doing…or, you should have seen what those twins in your first class did yesterday when they got out of the car. Hey, I saw a little boy that looked to be that boy in the paper the week before, that boy Jamie, was that the boy everyone thought would never walk again?"

Mr. Yancey knew my students almost as well as I did. He heard other people talk of the positive nature of the martial arts training I taught, there was always something good about our school in the local papers, and he never let a story about our students get past him.

"Mr. Tirschel," he'd say, "Come over when you get a chance, I have something for you." When I arrived he would hand me an article from the newspaper about one of my students that he cut out and saved for me.

It seemed as though Mr. Yancey was as much a part of my school as anyone.

One day though Mr. Yancey called me over because, as he put it, "I need to see you right away because I might have some bad news to tell you."

When I walked in he said solemnly, "Sit down Mr. Tirschel…it's that time you know."

"That time?" I wasn't sure what he meant.

He reminded me, "How long have you been renting from me now?"

"Oh yeah, we had a year lease and it's coming up isn't it?"

"We need to be talking about it now. You may need to make some plans."

"Yes sir."

"Well you know Mr. Tirschel, I can't continue to give you the same deal as we have been doing, prices go up you know."

"I understand sir."

"If you want to take the option for five more years, I'm going to have to raise the rent on you. Do you realize the $400 a month you're paying now is way below the market value for a space that size? That's 3500 sq ft. and look at the "location". You're right on the corner of this major intersection. I hope you understand I'm forced to raise the rent, that is, if you want to keep your studio here."

I sat quietly and as I waited to hear the "other shoe drop", I started contemplating what changes I'll have to make in order to keep teaching my students. I don't charge enough for the lessons, this is my first year here, and I teach too many economically challenged kids for free. I always knew I needed to be making more money.

I held my breath.

Then, apologetically, Mr. Yancey gave me the "bad" news, "I'm going to be forced to raise your rent to $425 a month if you want to stay Mr. Tirschel, it's up to you."

A five year lease written up for $425 a month. My feelings mixed wildly together. Would I be taking advantage of his lack of business sense, or is he supporting the purpose for which I conduct my service to these kids? At that time, I wasn't as sure as I am now what created this business option that was facing me. I wanted to shout "Great, no problem" but instead I just calmly said, "I understand Mr. Yancey, with the rate of inflation and all."

In the years to follow I visited him, as often as was comfortable for us both, and I would sit, and mostly listen to Mr. Yancey. Sometimes I had some news to contribute to his well-versed knowledge of the neighborhood, but listening to him discuss local business trends made it clear to me that his knowledge of economics and finance was way above me.

Every time I visited, his wife would answer the door and either say, "He's in his room…go on in" or "He's a little tired right now…he needs his rest."

In the third year of my wonderfully "negotiated" 5-year lease it was more often than not that my visits were turned away by Mr. Yancey's need to rest.

I never believed that it was I, that made such a sharp negotiated business deal, and that's why I continued to wave at that window, even though I knew Mr. Yancey no longer sat there, facing east on Forest Parkway.

5

There were several parking spaces directly in the front of my studio, but I parked in the back today. I wanted to get at the leaves that had a habit of collecting in the front of my studio, where people parked.

I walked around and unlocked the front door and checked for messages on my answering machine. There wasn't anything important, and so I went into the back of the studio to get a broom. When I came out from the back a tall skinny kid was standing just inside the front door.

His voice was tentative but still bold, "Sir…how much would it cost to take karate lessons here?"

"How old are you son?"

"I'm 12, sir."

"Can you bring your parents in with you sometime and I can lay it all out."

"No sir…I couldn't do that. How much would it cost me to take karate lessons here sir?"

His answer surprised me but he did get my attention. He seemed to possess a polite belligerence that remained focused on what he wanted, and what he would, or wouldn't be willing to give up getting it. I liked his confidence but there were certain procedures that I had to follow. He was a minor and I had to treat him as such.

I asked him "What's your name?"

"Stevie Carnes sir."

"Well Stevie Carnes…my name is Duke Tirschel." I shook his hand and added, "I'm glad to meet you Stevie."

"Yes Mr. Tirschel…me too sir"

"What's the problem of bringing your folks in Stevie?"

"I'd rather not say Mr. Tirschel…it's a long story."

"Just call me Duke…Stevie…just call me Duke."

"Yes sir."

"Stevie…I'll tell you what…" I threw him the broom, "if you sweep up outside and rake the leaves outback and agree to do some work around here when I need it…I'll trade the work you do for karate lessons…OK?"

"Yes sir…that's a deal Mr. Tirschel."

Before I could remind him to call me Duke he had turned to run outside and begin sweeping. "Wait a minute…" I called after him.

He turned "Yes sir?"

"Before you start class though, there is a paper you will have to take home and bring it backed signed by your parents…you have a problem with that?"

He was as skinny as a rail and stood taller than me and he acted like he was in the Marine Corps. With a bright beaming smile he yelled back, "No sir" and then went outside and got to work.

I liked that kid.

The phone was ringing and so I went to the wall phone in the work-out area and picked it up, "Thank you for calling; Tirschel Karate."

"Let me speak to Duke Tirschel please."

"This is Duke."

"Hi, this is Larry Ward."

"Yes Larry, what can I do for you?"

"Hey man this is Larry Ward, you know…Tasma the Magician."

"Well hey there Larry, how in the world are you? I'm sorry I didn't get that right away. I'm always calling you Tasma. I forgot you had a real name."

"Duke, I was checking back on the program for next month. I'm putting some new stuff together and I thought I'd check what themes you wanted me to emphasize during the show."

"Larry, let me get my notes. I'm going to get to my office, hold on."

I went to my office and pulled out my folder on Tasma the Magician and took out some notes I had worked on earlier in the week. "Here we are Larry" I picked the phone up and Larry and I worked out some positive mental attitude qualities I wanted him to institute into our bi-monthly magic show for the kids. I had been hiring Larry to reinforce the same principals and qualities with his magic that I have been teaching in class.

It's been a good way to get to the kids.

We've been doing the same thing for the adults by using James Metcalf the Hypnotist. It's just as effective and as much fun but for the adult classes. These were a couple of the tools I used that I feel had been responsible for our school growing so much.

We only had a small 3500 sq ft building but we had six hundred and five active students. That's because we were willing to hold full classes every day of the week and half a day Sunday. I never saw a school other than mine teach a full schedule of classes throughout the week including Friday and Saturday night from 4 pm in the afternoon until 10 pm at night.

Because of my personal success in operating my schools, I was asked to serve as the National Director for all the schools in the country affiliated with Chuck Norris. In the year after taking the position of National Director, our school was awarded the school of the year, and the following year, I was awarded Man of the Year by Chuck Norris.

It seemed as though everything we did in the karate school business flourished and my business and everything I did was a huge success.

A major goal in our school was to help youngsters feel good about their selves and to help them be able to handle conflicts in their lives, without thinking they have to fight in order to feel worthy. And when someone comes along who can't afford the classes we find something they can do so they can be a part of our program.

"All done Mr. Tirschel," Stevie was back just inside the front door holding the rack.

"Did you do the back parking lot?"

"Yes sir, and the side driveway between the buildings."

I checked around back and on the sides. He did what he said, and so I sat down with Stevie, gave him a schedule of the classes, and told him I would have a uniform for him when he came for his first class.

"Stevie, bring that release of liability form…that's this one," I pulled it out of the pack of papers I gave him and laid it on top, "have your parents sign this and bring it back with you."

"Yes sir."

There was something about this kid that told me he needed a break somewhere in life. And when I saw his face light up from the achievement of going after something he wanted, and getting it, I was so happy for him. Although I didn't know a thing about this kid, I was proud of how he handled himself.

How great it made me feel; to imagine that I might be able to hold out a hand and steady the boy who was trying to become a man.

With that last thought I fell asleep. But whatever had a hold of my life blinded me, and I couldn't see just where it was, that I jumped the track.

6

I thought, and slept, and dreamt, and woke. And after that entire process, I saw that only twenty minutes had gone by. I was amazed at how deeply I could fall asleep and how well rested I could be, without fully leaving the state of being awake. We call that a "power nap"; falling so deep into sleep that you were so totally rested, in such an extremely, short period of time.

I opened my eyes and stared out at the lights of the cars speeding by, on the freeway, on the other side of the chain link fence.

I felt the vibration of my cell phone before it started ringing.

"Yeah?"

"This you...Duke?"

"Who's this?"

"Spider."

"Yeah...what's up man?"

"Back me up...where you at?"

"The Palace...what do you need?"

"Go down to Happy's...stop Rooster if he comes out the back."

"What's going down?"

"Rooster gave my girl a hot load...bout killed her. I'm going to see that she gets him back. I don't want him running though. I'm going to make him stand up and fight, you know Theresa. She's tough. She'll smash his face in."

I said, "Heading that way".

I pulled out of the lot, went past Connell Street, took a left onto Cleveland avenue, and then a quick right onto the freeway. I was fifteen minutes away from Happy's game room, and although I didn't rush, I went straight there as I said I would.

When I was two blocks away from Happy's, I saw Spider's car coming towards me on Old Dixie highway. It wasn't until I saw a flash from Spiders car, and heard a single popping sound of a nine millimeter being fired, that I saw a man running across the grass in front of a huge store that sold motor boats. He ran a few more steps, after the gunshot, and then without another shot fired, he fell. Spider's car turned at the corner and disappeared into the dark street separating two industrial warehouses. His car was swallowed up by the darkness, which meant he must have turned off his headlights. I did the same, and dove into the darkness after him. Way down the block in the distance, against a wall of darkness, I saw a red tail light just for a moment. He had to either go left or right because the street ended at the front yard of someone's house there. I didn't know which way he went, and so I decided to just get as far away as I could.

I was on the freeway heading for the north side when my phone rang, "Yeah?"

"Where were you man?"

"Spider?"

"What took you so long? I had to chase him down man. He ran out the back and I had to chase him."

"I thought Theresa was going to…"

"She was. But I thought the back was covered.'

"I went straight there. Why didn't you wait for me?"

"Theresa lost her temper and jumped him."

"How'd he give her a hot load anyway…don't you test your stuff?"

"His stuff ain't like that normally. He usually cuts the hell out of it, and he knows she shoots up. She thinks he did it on purpose."

I said, "So you shot him?"

"You got a problem with that?"

"I don't, but…you, we still have a lot of work to do, man. But now, you're going to have to go underground for a while. I can't use you now."

"What about Hot Rod? I can still set that up for you."

"I'm going to kick that back to Rocky…the last time I talked to him he said he would set Hot Rod up for me. He just wants me to wait until Hot Rod pays what he owes him. You need to go under for awhile, you know. See what happens with Rooster. Where do you think you hit him?"

"I was aiming for the back of his head but I think I got him in middle of his back."

"I imagine people saw you chase him from Happy's?"

"Yeah, so what?"

"Spider! Go somewhere for a while. See if Rooster makes it…or whatever."

I changed my mind about going to the other side of town. No one saw me, and Spider's probably going to go out and stay with Rocky. I was coming up on Moreland Ave. so I pulled off and headed for Tommy's place.

Tommy dated my daughter for a while and he seemed to be a pretty decent guy. We became good friends and remained friends after they broke it off. Tommy was married now and had a little girl. He managed Tara's, a game room across from Flanagan's, a strip joint out on Moreland Avenue, far from the center of Atlanta. Many of the patrons of Flanagan's, like most strip joints around town, were underage and sported authentic ID's.

It's not that the club cares that anyone's too young to be in the bar as long as they have possession of an ID that says they're not underage. But the manager of the club has to know that you can be trusted not to ditch the ID if the club gets raided. Since the girls can work in a strip club three years before they are allowed to drink, there are a lot of underage issues going on.

By the time I arrived at Tara's, the last of the crowd at Flanagan's across the street was leaving, and coming over to prolong the night. Like all the other game rooms in Atlanta, Tara's open 24 hours a day, 7 days a week. They don't serve alcohol but there are always a couple bottles of booze in the office reserved for "regulars".

But it's rare that anyone cares for a drink with the crowd that stays up this long.

A typical game room is an empty shell of a building, or retail space less than 1000 sq ft. in size. Electronic games line the walls with a tall stool sitting in front of each machine. The light level in the room is low to no light, at all. The darkness mixes with the blue and green lights fluorescing off the screens, and gives you an eerie feeling.

But it's the sounds that stay with you; the audible commands of the machines and the gongs ringing like the sound of pinball machines. Occasionally, there's a voice above the normal hush that yells out because of something huge being won.

You won't hear a burst of sound at anything huge being lost, because that never happens. The machines don't let you lose in big chunks. It would be too noticeable that way. Instead it gives you an occasional big win and then it continues to take just a little back at a time. But the little bit it takes from you, it takes over a long period of time, and you never see it go. You just lose track of time and before you know it, you're busted.

The truck driver killing time, a desperate housewife or a single mother, or too often a business man trying to recoup the wages he spent in a bar the night before, these are the patrons of the game room. There are no professional gamblers here, just suckers trying to get lucky.

"Just one time and never again."

They'll lose their paycheck, their grocery money, and whatever cash money their little family has put away for an emergency.

Gambling is illegal in Georgia and so the players are playing for the prizes that are displayed in a glass case behind the bar where soft drinks and hot dogs are sold. The prizes could range from anything from a pocketknife to an upscale video camera.

It really doesn't matter what the prize is, because the prizes in the case will do nothing but gather dust. Players accumulate points that appear to go towards obtaining the prizes, but in reality, those points represent cash payouts that far exceed the cost of the prizes in the showcase.

Some of the overflow from Flanagan's might play the games while they're at Tara's, but there are also a few pool tables to kill time on, and some couches where die-hard party people can hang out and do their dope. It would really be tough on a dope dealer if there were no place to go this early in the morning and it would even be worse for the dealers selling speed, if there were no reason to stay awake. So they play pool, foosball and if all else fails, just hang out, anything but go home and go to bed.

When you're doing speed you just get too bored cleaning the house all night or rearranging your sock drawer, so you go hang out at the game room and do whatever comes down the pike. If you were near an all-night Wal-Mart, you could browse for hours on end, now that would take preference over all.

Speed does funny things to one's thinking and so anything that can be done all-night (and most of the next day) is all right. Game rooms are open 24/7, and they are the place people regroup while getting, the next thing to be done, started.

Tommy was running Tara's and worked for a friend of ours who owned several game rooms, and affiliated with most of the other ones in town.

Tommy wasn't in the game room tonight but when he found out I was there, he called and asked me to come by his house. Before we even sat down he made me an offer. "Hey man, want to make some extra cash?"

"What do you got in mind?"

"I was talking to Brian last night and he suggested I approach you with a deal. You know Brian, he has a lot of these game rooms and he was talking to Mike and Gene and a few of the others."

I listened.

Tommy's wife Lisa is a pretty brunette who used to dance at Tattletales, a strip club known for their beautiful dancers. She quit dancing and now is quite the homebody housewife and the perfect mother. She came in and sat on the arm of Tommy's easy chair.

Tommy put his arm around her waist and with his other hand he picked up her arm and kissed the back of her hand. Looking up at her he said, "Baby, would you go fix us something."

"What do you want Sweetheart?"

"Oh just anything...anything will be alright. We'll be through here in a minute."

I was wondering if Tommy was hungry or if he wanted Lisa to bring him a drink. The question just crossed my mind quickly but it was no big thing. It was just that the request he made was a bit confusing to me.

Lisa didn't go into the kitchen. She leisurely walked down the hallway, stopped and quietly opened the door to their little girl's room and stuck her head in. She had a smile on her face when she came back out and looked down the hallway towards us. She put her finger across her lips in a "shushing" mode and then tiptoed down the hallway and went into their bedroom and quietly closed the door.

What a kind couple these two were to each other.

What I had just seen told me that Tommy was getting ready to talk business, and instead of sending his wife off in a rude way, he was asking for some privacy.

He picked up where he left off, "It's hard to keep these rooms operating 24 hours a day. We get some young kid or a girl to work there at odd hours and we're just asking for trouble. We've been getting hit by a bunch of punks."

"Hit?"

"Yeah, they know whose working where and when. They know who'll look the other way or who would be too scared not to. The punks come in and break open the machines and take the money. Sometimes they do it without the girl knowing it by crowding around a machine and play it and make a lot of noise like they're just having fun while one of them is jimmying the machine. And sometimes they come in and just smash the machines and grab the money and run."

"Do you call the cops?"

"Duke…we can't call the cops, too many issues…they would close us down. They're just looking for an excuse."

"So what are you going to do?"

"We were talking of hiring you. Your presence alone around the rooms would deter them. But once you make an example of one of them they'd stay away."

I had known Tommy and all these guys for a long time but these kids are half my age and they don't know my standards. They see me with low-life but they don't see me. They think I'll do anything at anytime fro any reason. It's hard for me to get the idea across to them that I see myself as being "in the water" but I don't see myself as being "of the water."

"Gee whiz, Tommy. We've known each other a long time." I hesitated as I thought of whether I should try to explain it to him. "You know me, I think funny, man. You know."

I guess he didn't know because he frowned and shook his head, "What do you mean? You turning Godly on us or something? I heard you go to those big meetings and stuff?"

"You mean Promise Keepers, yeah man, it's awesome. It would be neat if all our guys would…aw, maybe not."

Tommy said, "Hey, I used to go to church, really. When Tessie gets a little older we're going to start up again."

"That's cool."

"So that's it huh? You going all bible on us, boy?"

"It's not like that."

"Well, how about helping us out with these punks, then?"

"Tommy, of course I think what those guys are doing to you is bad. I wish they weren't doing it…and…I'm not above anyone else…don't get me wrong. But when I go in a game room, in the middle of the day, and see a mother hooked on trying to make a little extra money, and see her lose what money she has for groceries, it bothers me."

"It doesn't bother them when they take our money. They're just looking for a shortcut. Why feel sorry for them?"

"I don't feel sorry for them, but my heart couldn't get into helping anyone who feeds off them."

"So you're against gambling?"

"Tommy? That's not gambling. These game rooms aren't attracting heavy hitting gamblers. They're milking a little at a time from poor people, and that "little" is a lot to them. They just have stupid dreams of striking it rich."

"Ok," Tommy shrugged, "We thought we'd ask…"

"It's not a moral issue Tommy."

"That's alright…that's Ok…"

"No…hear me out…"

"That's alright, I understand."

"No. You don't Tommy. I would lose."

"What do you mean…lose?"

"Look, if some huge guy, say some professional fighter, or a professional killer, doesn't matter. If I had to go against someone like that and I was in the right…if I felt right in my own heart…there is no way I could lose. I really believe that, I truly do. But on the other hand, if I faced a four-year old little girl on crutches, and I was in the wrong, or if I did not feel right about what I was doing…if I didn't have my heart in it, that little girl would crush me like a paper cup. That's what I believe. It's not what I think in my head, it's what I believe in my heart that determines what I do."

Tommy leaned forward and took a quick look over his shoulder and said, "Ok I can buy that. Maybe then, you can do something just for me."

"Do what?"

Tommy checked one more time over his shoulder, "Lisa's 'ex' is a part of that bunch from Cabbage Town doing the rooms. I don't think it's so much for the money, but this guy Haney, Lisa's 'ex', is doing it out of spite, to get back at her for leaving him. He used to beat the hell out of her and now he's got her scared to death."

"What do you want?"

"Forget about the rooms, run up on Haney, and you know, change his thinking. The crap going on with the rooms will stop…but no, forget about the rooms. It's not for the game rooms. All I want is for Haney to quit scaring Lisa."

"That's different. Of course I will."

"I would appreciate it personally, you know?"

"I know…but do you understand where I'm coming from? This makes all the difference in the world. I'll go after him for what he's doing to you and your family. If it works out that your game rooms get cut some slack, well then, it just works out that way."

7

Being fully awake and alert in the middle of the night when everyone else was asleep gave me a sense of power. It was like I had something other people didn't have; I had a bigger slice of life and I wasn't wasting it conked out in the back of the house somewhere.

I was on the move and after seeing Tommy, I'd easily be up for several days, wide awake and no fuzzy thinking. My mind was racing and my thoughts quickened and my needs were that of action. After all, that's why they call it 'speed'.

Moreland Avenue ran north and south. Tara's was on that part of Moreland that extended south outside the major freeway that circled Atlanta and past all the trucker depots and deep into redneck country.

I was going back to Tara's so as I could begin getting the word out that I'm looking for Haney. The night was pitch black on either side, for a couple miles down the road. The road slowly began lighting up as I approached the intersection where a well lit building, surrounded by a nearly empty parking lot, sat off to the left and a smaller blue building sat off to the right.

"Hey Gina…whatzup?"

Gina gave me hug, "This job is just temporary Duke. Nicky let me go again."

"Sorry to hear that, I thought you left Nicky's a long time ago."

Gina nodded towards a machine in the far corner, "Hey there's Mark. Been here for three days."

Besides selling it, Mark was more hooked on his own product than any of his clients. I nodded in his direction, "Must have some pretty good stuff…huh?"

"You know Mark. It's some good go…why? You looking?" Gina tapped her nose and gave a short sniff. "See me first."

"I'm fine. Hey, listen Gina; I'm looking for a guy from Cabbage Patch by the name…"

"You mean Cabbage Town?"

"They're a bunch of punks, I call it Cabbage Patch. The guy I'm looking for, his name is Haney. You know him?"

"Oh he's a real freak, I know him. Tommy married his…"

"I know. Just let the word out for him to get in touch with me. Get it around that he better find me before I find him, and I will find him. So…say, well just say I want to talk to him, that's all. Here's my number." I gave her the number to my cell phone and said, "Back in a minute" and walked over to Mark.

"Hey bro, you breaking the bank yet?"

Mark was popping in twenties as fast as he could while playing three machines at a time. I never played these machines so I couldn't tell by all the bells and whistles whether he was doing any good or not.

The fact that he was still there must mean something. I just didn't know what it was. "Hey Duke…I just hit Cherries across man and have a good run going on this one over here…sit down…play awhile.'

"I wouldn't begin to know how to do that."

"Hey Duke, see that girl playing pool? Her sister goes with Scott. She and that guy have been here for three days that I know, maybe more. I've been here for three and they were here when I got here."

"Who's the guy?"

"Never saw him before, never seen her before either. But check it out, she just come out and said she was a prostitute. Do you believe that? Yeah that's right man, and that was her boyfriend and she was supporting the two of them, but he's too jealous and won't let her work. They don't have a car, a place to stay, and I haven't seen them eat anything for three days."

"The Kings Inn is in walking distance. Why don't they…"

"Oh yes, and they ain't got no money. Gina's been letting them play pool for free and I give her a line once in awhile and she tries to pay for it with her…"

"Oh come on Mark, don't tell me you would take…"

"No man, I didn't."

"Look at her Mark. How old would you say? She doesn't look to be but 16 or 17."

"Says she's 25."

"Hmm really? Interesting…" I smiled and punched Mark's shoulder lightly, "Let me go see if she can play pool." I walked across the room to their pool table and put four quarters on the edge of the table.

The girl said, "The table's open, Gina's letting us play free." She smiled, "But you can put that dollar towards a coke and you can play now. Jack and I are just messing around here."

"If he's Jack who are you?"

"I'm Britney."

"I'm Duke. Rack 'em I'll get you a coke."

She was a pretty good pool player and she thinks she beat me but I think her count was wrong. She started to give me a play-by-play description of every game we played with such authority I started to doubt myself and so before she gave proof that she did beat me I said, "Oh well, go ahead…you win…it doesn't matter to me."

"Really?"

"Yeah, it's just a game. I can lose to a girl, it doesn't matter to me."

I was tired of playing pool but there wasn't anything else to do and I didn't want to leave just yet. If anything at all I was intrigued by her. She had a very pretty face and although she was a little plump, her weight seemed to add an element of something sensual. The innocent manner in which she bragged of working as a prostitute on 3rd street, since she was 14 years old, made me disbelieve that she could be anything like she said she was. The "working girls" I knew didn't tell every stranger they met.

If anything at all, I wanted to talk to her and find out what is in the head of this pretty little miss-placed phenomenon. "I need to go home. Can I drop you two anywhere?"

She answered so directly that I believe she knew the intent of my question, "We don't have no place to go."

I feigned my surprise, "What? No place to go? What do you mean?"

"We've been here, probably…maybe four days now. My sister left me here. Her and Tank took off and there's no telling when they'll get back."

"Well you two can stay at my place. Call them from there if you want to."

"OK…that would be…"

Jack jumped in and eyed me suspiciously, "No that's alright. We'll wait here."

Britney wrinkled her nose, made a frowning face and whispered an objection to Jack. Then, she turned to me, "It's Ok…we'll go." She got behind Jack, put her hands on each of his arms and turned him towards the corner, "My stuff's over there", gave a little push and Jack went and fetched it.

What "it" consisted of was everything Britney owned in the world.

"It" all fit in a large black garbage bag.

8

The next three days were spent at my house in Marietta. I lived in a spacious three-bedroom duplex with a two-car garage and a huge basement, a back patio, a front porch and a huge living room with a vaulted ceiling and a fireplace.

I lived there alone. There was plenty of room.

Occasionally, in the three days they were there, I left the house and went in search of Haney and left word for him at places he might be, and then waited to see if someone would call and rat him out. I knew he wouldn't be calling me. Calls came in that he was seen at one place or the other, but I would call someone I knew at that location and check it out, before wasting my time making a trip there.

None of the information panned out. I was hoping that he would surface soon because I had a photography job in Canada. I would be driving there and I'd be leaving Atlanta as soon as I could.

Before I left I would need to take Jack and Britney and drop them off somewhere. I was curious about and every time we would get a chance to talk Jack would walk in and Britney would quit talking. I went to my office in one part of the house, Britney followed, and we began talking, and minutes later, Jack would walk in. Later, I went down to my Art and Graphics section in the basement, and Britney followed, and minutes later, Jack would show up again.

Finally, I told Britney I needed her help flush Haney out of the Taj Mahal, a strip club a few blocks away. I told Jack I need him to stay near the phone and wait for a call from us, with instructions for him to call the Taj Mahal and ask for Haney. He objected vehemently, but Britney hollered at him, we got our way, and left the house together.

We went down the street to a sports bar and ordered a couple beers.

Britney said, "I thought we were going to the Taj Mahal."

"I just wanted to get away from your boyfriend."

"He's not my boyfriend. He lives next door to my parents' house. He's had a crush on me since grade school. I just can't get rid of him. I quit school in the six grade and got rid of him for a while, but when I visit my folks he finds out where I'm staying, and starts it up all over again."

"Starts what up?

"He follows me everywhere and thinks he's my boyfriend."

"Why don't you just tell him to leave you alone?"

"I do. But it hurts his feelings and, he's really not so bad to bum around with. But he's not a boyfriend."

"Britney, have you ever been to Canada?"

"Why?"

"Would you like to go?"

"You mean with you and that job you have to do?"

"Yeah."

"Jack too."

"No."

"OK."

It was set. That is what I wanted. I could use the company getting there and she might be helpful on the job.

We rushed back to my house and since I was already packed, we loaded the trunk with my stuff and threw Britney's black garbage bag in the back seat. We told Jack that we were all going to go somewhere for a few days.

I wasn't sure how we were going to play it. We wanted to get rid of Jack but we didn't want to leave him in a bad way. I drove to the Days Inn over on Delk Road. I reached into the back seat and handed Jack a $100 bill and told him to get us a room. "Tell them that it's one person so it will be cheaper and once you have the room we'll sneak in."

The minute he entered the office I threw the car in reverse and backed-up. Jack was out the door immediately. Britney screamed, "Oh no…here he comes."

Jack ran at us like a cartoon figure. His hands were waving frantically and he was yelling, "Wait…Wait."

He blocked the direction I was going to go so I turned the car in the other direction and decided to go completely around the building. I saw him take off running back towards the office. As I accelerated through the parking area, of the other side of the building, I saw why Jack ran back towards the office. He cut through a walkway of the building that led to the other side. Standing out in the middle of the parking lot, he held his arms out as if he were going to tackle the car. I hit the brakes and spun the car back in the other direction. He turned back to the walkway, where he just came out, and started running to the other side. As soon as he disappeared into the walkway, on his way to the other side of the building, I spun the car around again and continued in the direction I was going. By the time I turned the corner at the far end of the building, I saw that Jack was quick to figure out that we doubled back, because now, he was running to this end of the building.

Britney was laughing as she let out a loud scream.

She got on her knees and started bouncing up and down on the seat as she looked out the back window and yelled, "Hurry…hurry…here he comes."

I looked behind us and he was already at our rear bumper. I floored the accelerator and we pulled away, but we had to slow down again, to turn and pull out of the parking lot. He saw where we were heading, and so he cut at an angle and ran towards the spot where we would come out on to the street. Again, he was in front of us, and so I cut sharply to the right and gunned it down Delk Road. I saw him running down the middle of the road, with legs and arms flailing away. As this comedic figure grew smaller and smaller in my rear view mirror, I started feeling sorry for Jack.

I felt sorry for Jack because now, I know him.

For the last few days Jack had been around me constantly. I've talked to him and I talked to Britney about him. I thought I had him figured out, but now I see him as a totally different person, and I felt sorry for him because; now, I believe I really knew him.

Jack was twenty-five years old, but he was just an over grown kid. He didn't work because he didn't have a trade, a skill, or an education. He didn't even appear as though he had a desire to have any of that. When Britney quit school in the 6th grade and left home, Jack quit school too. Britney worked as a prostitute and Jack lived off of her until Britney fell in love with someone else and Jack had to go home. All of his life, Jack lived with an alcoholic grandmother who never asked Jack why he wasn't in school.

I knew these things about Jack but I didn't know Jack, not until now.

Jack was a puppy dog. He didn't really love, not as much as he desperately needed to be petted, so that he would feel loved himself.

I know Jack.

I've been Jack.

I've done exactly what Jack did tonight. As a matter of fact, that was me, I was being Jack tonight. By my running away from Jack, I was running towards Britney just as hard as he was tonight. It was no difference just because I was inside the car.

I was flailing my hands and arms and shoulders, and with my heels coming way up behind me, I was running as wildly as Jack was. Both of us were gangly inexperienced kids, throwing every bit of ourselves towards what we were trying to catch, and I wound up with what we were chasing.

I imagined what Jack would do once my car was out of sight.

He would turn around, slowly open his fist, and discover a crumpled piece of paper in his hand. The warm humid air would carry a gentle breeze, and this would produce the coolness that would bring to Jack's attention, he was sweating. The level of work his running produced would have him sit down on the curb, exhausted.

One lone streetlight would loom like a giant over the small figure, resting on the side of the road, at three o'clock in the morning. There would be no cars, parked or moving, in sight. There is just a wide empty road, lined with darkened store windows just waiting for the next day's run at glory.

Everything, about the night, ignored the tired young man sitting on the curb, looking at the hundred dollar bill in his hand. He will probably press out the wrinkles of the bill, carefully, by flattening it on his leg, and quickly forget what he traded for it.

It would then dawn on him that this hundred-dollar bill was all his and he would marvel at all the things he could buy with it. And then, just like a small child who suddenly forgot why he was crying, he would stand up and begin to walk home.

He would get back to his grandmother's house and wait for Britney. She would come back around again; Jack was sure of it.

9

We jumped on I-75 North, in Atlanta, and headed to Toronto, Canada.

We stopped four times for gas, and once at 2 am the next morning, we stopped to browse an Adult Book Store. We needed to stretch our legs and such. Other than that, we drove straight through. No sleep was needed. There was too much to talk about.

Britney was intrigued with my life of movies, stunt work, karate, and even the "security" work I do for select individuals on the street. I was equally intrigued with her life.

Being "taken" in and "cared" for, she fell in love with her black pimp who treated her well as long as she was making money. He put her up in a cheap motel with a few other girls and paid all her bills and gave her a little spending money. He lived in a nice house, drove a big car, and had a beautiful wife. He told Britney that someday he would get rid of his wife and Britney would move in with him. But she had to work hard and make a lot of money for that to happen. Britney fell in love with the thought of having a home.

We didn't stop telling each other the secrets we had about ourselves, once we got to Canada. The fact that we were there had nothing to do with us. We had no control over the synergistic forces that we were building between the two of us. Britney helped set up my photography equipment, and while we were setting up, we paid no attention to anyone else who might be listening, as we talked. When we finished work, we declined going out to dinner with the instructor. We went back to the motel, talked through the night, and into the next day, until it was time to go to the next school and set up the backdrop and lights, and shoot photos of the students at that school.

In between, shooting each student, we continued talking.

We did that for a week. I don't remember our schedule, or how we found each of the karate schools we were to photograph. I don't remember the students I photographed, or the instructors we didn't go to dinner with. But I remembered talking about my life, and her life, and how life would be for both of us, if we were together.

One night, before we headed back to the States, I gave in to what we argued about the most. I finally agreed with her about us, but I didn't really know what I was in agreement with.

There's magic in that phrase, "I love you" that makes us answer with, "I love you too."

What a great feeling to be in love, or even, just to think you are. When I fall in love I pretend the other person really does love me, even though I know the words "I love you" don't always mean what they say.

But this time, Wow! Yes, this time she played her part well.

She actually *was* too young for me. But with tears in her eyes she said I was wrong to think our age difference could have anything to do with how she felt about me. She told me that no one had ever been as understanding about her feelings as I had been.

Then there was her lifestyle.

She told me that other men she dated would beat her up and throw her out once they found out she was a prostitute.

So, I read her a verse from the bible.

It was John 8: 2-11 which tells about the time Jesus was teaching in the temple when the Pharisees brought in a woman caught in the act of adultery. They asked Him, "Teacher, in the Law, Moses commanded us to stone such women, what do you say?"

Jesus answered by saying, "Let the one who is without sin cast the first stone." And slowly, one by one, starting with the oldest, each one of the Pharisees left and there only remained Jesus and this woman. When Jesus saw that there was no one left except the two of them, He said, "Woman, where are they? Has no one condemned you?"

"No one, sir" she said.

"Then neither do I condemn you," Jesus declared. "Go and sin no more"

And, when I finished reading this to her, I looked up, and saw tears streaming down her face, "Help me would you? Like that woman there in the bible…you know like she did and not sin no more…you know…like that."

From that point on I was hooked.

She was twenty-five years old and had been a prostitute for eleven years. She never went past the sixth-grade in school, and she still had that eleven year-old look of wonder in her eye. But on a dark downtown street at three in the morning, she was a "pro", and she could wrap you around her little finger and send you away totally spent, and as equally broke.

She knew her way around on the streets at night, but in the light of day she was a twenty-five year old chubby little girl, who looked like an eleven year-old ditching school. She looked and acted like she should be sitting in the principal's office, at a Junior High School, waiting to be reprimanded for ditching class.

I was totally sincere in my thoughts of "saving" this girl from the "street".

Although I had no idea of what I was doing, my plan was to save her by bringing her to God; and for doing so, I expected her to be filled with so much gratitude that she would be eternally faithful to me. I found a flawed person that no one else wanted. I would fix her and that would make her mine.

I could "help" her by taking away the wild nightlife, help her get rid of the drugs and the alcohol, and keep her from having to be around all those young good-looking guys, her own age, who just wanted her for the wild excitement, they were so good at providing each other.

I thought if I could show her that I valued having her in my life she might begin to sense a value for herself, just by my being there, and maybe then, she'd do whatever she could to stay there. But the down side of the plan was that I secretly hoped that her self-worth would only grow to the point that she would leave the life she had with others, and that she would give it all to me.

If we could have grasped what would eventually happen to us, we would have left Canada with a different plan. But as fate would have it, when we crossed the border heading back to Atlanta, our lives were totally changed from what they were the week before.

We were "in love" or at least we said we were, and I for one, believed us both.

Before heading south, we stopped at the bowling alley lockers, in Buffalo, New York, where we kept our 'stash' and my Mossberg and the shoulder holster with my 44 Bulldog. We didn't want to take the chance of being stopped with any of this at the border crossing.

We had no sooner pulled out of the parking lot of the bowling alley in Buffalo that I received a call on my cell phone, "Hello."

"Duke?"

"Who's this?"

"This is Tommy…Duke?"

"Yeah man, how's it going?"

Tommy laughed, "Oh…you know. Nothing going on here, at all." And then he laughed again but louder this time. "Duke…you're de man."

I smiled.

Tommy said, "It worked out a lot better than I thought it would."

"Great." I didn't know what was so great but I figured he was rockin' on something and so why bust his high, "I'm glad you're happy…can't wait until I get back. I want what ever you're on."

Tommy said, "You can have anything you want".

Britney tapped me on the shoulder and pointed to the freeway sign that said, "Buffalo left lane".

I nodded, "Thanks baby."

"Hey Tommy…I can have anything?"

"You name it."

"How about your Corvette?"

"You serious?"

"Tommy…of course I'm not serious. So whatzup, why you so "giving" all of a sudden?"

"You know…Haney…hey hold a minute I got a call coming in…"

I turned to Britney, "You hungry?"

She nodded and pointed to a McDonalds sign.

When Tommy came back on the line, I said, "Look we're getting something to eat. I'll check back with you...but what's this thing about Haney?"

"Well...the poor guy got shot last Saturday night."

"Dead?"

"No, but he sure has changed his attitude."

"Who did it?"

Tommy laughed, "Gee Duke...I just can't figure that one out."

"Oh no..." I was shaking my head. "Not me...we left for Canada on Friday night and you said he was shot...when...on Saturday, right?"

"That's right Duke;" you can hear the smile in his voice "couldn't have been you could it? Come on in when you get back and we'll settle up."

"Hey Tommy..."

"Got to go man. Someone's on the other line. I just wanted to call and say nice job, and hey Duke, Lisa and I, we both thank you, man."

The line went dead.

I pulled into McDonalds, parked the car and sat there for a couple minutes thinking, whether or not, I would explain the conversation to Britney.

10

By the time we reached Atlanta, we decided on the roles we would take, so that we could 'help' each other. Britney would move in with me, she would help me with my business, and I would take care of her.

It was a twisted rope, in which our lives got tangled, once this young prostitute got hooked up with me. We designed a relationship that said she was my roommate, and we dated other people, yet professed to love each other.

There was no safety in this relationship, for neither of us, nor was there anyway of fixing anything that gone wrong. My goal was to provide a home for Britney so that she wouldn't have to live on the street as a prostitute. But, she continued with her bizarre sex life that I tried to counsel her against, not as a boyfriend or lover, but as a roommate, and a friend.

But still, I was surprised at the feelings of jealousy that began to possess me.

I began missing work and repeatedly failed to make my appointments on time. When I was away from this woman, I felt an agonizing painful fear in my gut. As hard as I tried, I could not concentrate on the service I owed to those with whom I did business.

When I was around her, our lives were filled with unanswered questions over which we fought incessantly. We began to abuse each other to the extent that we could no longer tell which one of us was the victim.

My focus, on any productive course in life, was blurred by my possessive behavior over Britney. But productivity worsened even more because of the reactions concerning the Haney shooting.

The day we returned from Canada, Tommy tried to pay me for shooting Haney, but I refused to take it. And as time went on, I thought it wouldn't hurt anything if I quit refusing to accept the credit for having done the deed. I didn't take any money from Tommy for it, but I let everyone believe what they wanted to believe. I never said I did it, but I quit saying I didn't. He wasn't hurt all that much anyway and it sure put me in a light that swelled my head among the low life.

The jacking of the game rooms stopped and the owners of the clubs believed it was because of me.

My popularity increased to a ridiculous level.

There wasn't a game room, or a club, where someone didn't approach me with a bizarre job. I didn't even know the people who came up to me, and they all had the most lame brain requests. But I listened to their half-baked schemes, and I let them drag my ego up on their pedestal. In most cases I said, "Give me a number and I'll look into it." But rarely did I just say, "No".

A construction worker filing for divorce didn't want his wife to show up at court. "Any way at all that you want to handle it is fine. I just don't want her showing up."

Another stranger says, "I'm divorced and my wife has custody of my son. The guy my 'ex' is dating is beating my kid. I want him hurt…bad."

Another one says, "This jerk shows up at my place of business everyday and flirts with my wife who helps me. I can't do anything…it would be bad for business. I want you to be like you're just a customer and he bumps into you. He can't know it's coming from me but I want him hurt right there in front of my wife. She can't know either."

While in any club, I could look up from my place at the bar, and see the eyes watching me. Strangers, I never saw before, but they heard about me. Those watching eyes were the way people stood in line to see me; to get done what it is they think I do. They were waiting their turn. As soon as the last guy left, and I tucked his number in my pocket, the next pair of watching eyes would approach with his proposition. "Listen, there's a couple guys that hang out at Spondivits and they always give me a bad time when I go in there…it's embarrassing…and I got the hots for one of the girls there…how much would you charge to just walk in with me, have a few drinks and then we leave together?"

"What for?"

"I just want them to see that I know you and…you know…that I'm a friend of yours…or something."

So many eyes waiting for their turn to bring me some simple common little evil deed to do…and frankly, I loved it.

When no one else was looking I thought to myself, "I'm the man" and then when I caught another pair of watchful eyes waiting, I nodded and they approached with their pathetic story, "I think my wife is cheating on me. I think I know who it is…I can't afford to pay you to do surveillance, I don't care about that. I'm pretty sure I know who it is…what would it cost just to go ahead and hurt the guy I think it is?"

I didn't take the jobs the nine-to-fivers wanted done. I just listened from my pedestal and most of the time advised them against what they said they wanted to have done. For the most part, what they really wanted was someone to advise them against doing what they professed they wanted done. They wanted to be talked out of hurting someone. It makes the nine-to-fiver feel powerful to pretend they were serious about getting someone hurt. And, by checking into getting someone's legs broken, proves that they were the real deal and that they meant business.

But, for the most part they were relieved that I wouldn't do what they asked of me. Just that they thought they could hurt, who was hurting them; that was enough. To openly entertain the violence, they said they wanted done, was the limit to their striking back.

I've learned a long time ago, you don't hurt some guy because his wife pays you to do it, or because she convinced you of the terrible way she's been treated. As soon as the husband is laying on the ground the woman, who paid you to put him there, will run to him and turn against you. It's very much the same in all the propositions you get from a nine-to-fiver; they go soft and back out on the deal they make with you.

The jobs I did take were to collect money from 'bad' debts connected with gambling, and drug deals. All this carving of a new "career" was being done while I was bent on fixing what was wrong with my life. I saw Britney as the core of my problems, and so I wanted any kind of work that kept me in town, so I could keep my eye on her.

I tried to camouflage the possessiveness I had over Britney, with the image I tried to project of 'saving' a young girl, from all those "bad" people in the world that would do her harm.

One wrong decision after another, and a consistent run of "family" disturbances, drew attention of our lifestyle to the local police departments. All I can remember now, was the shootings, the police, the arrests, and the blood, and the lives that were shattered, once I was convinced that I needed to save this young girl from everyone, but me.

But after all, we only did what we knew to do, there's no need to blame either of us for being insane. Neither of us were who we thought we were. After all, when I met her I was really being introduced to everyone whose influence had contributed to who she became. When I met her I was introduced to parents, stepparents, foster parents, teachers, preachers, and pimps.

Anyone who ever affected the way I thought was here to meet her when she met me. Because just by her knowing me she came to know parole officers, cell mates, enemies, best friends, girl friends, past lovers, and last date.

But, because I didn't know who I was, we were both brought face to face, with an unknown part of me. One day I asked a friend of mine, "Why would a 6'8" 340 pound bouncer be afraid of me."

She laughed as though it was such a stupid question, "Well Duke…it's because they just never know what you're going to do."

I thought about that for a long time, and then admitted, "You know what? Neither do I."

11

In the months that followed, my photography business fell off, and gave way to the senseless "jobs" I chose from the "street". I found myself in and out of jail for the most ridiculous charges.

When not behind bars, I and the collection of lost souls in my life, blended into the dark places of night. We lurked just around corners one doesn't normally care to look. Even the most street wise were shocked whenever we stepped from the shadows and let our presence be felt. There was never anything good to come from anywhere we went, and we were always on our way to trouble.

Time meant nothing in the way we lived our lives.

Our days didn't start or end on purpose, nor was there even a purpose for our day. There wasn't a time it started or a time it ended. When life gave us four, five, or six days without sleep, we just fell out wherever we were at the time, and didn't worry where that was or where we were supposed to be. We just pulled the plug and closed our eyes.

Time meant nothing, and so any measure of it, wasn't kept too closely as a rule.

But one night, that all changed.

I was at the house asleep when I heard the pounding on my door followed by another flurry of loud knocks and someone shouting, "Duke, we know you're in there, open up, Cobb County Police, we want to talk to you."

Immediately, time took on a different hue. Time looked more important than I'd ever seen it look before. The measure of time was suddenly critical.

I thought about the length of time since I was last arrested, and how much time had passed since I was released on bond. There was the regret for the time that I wasted in getting things cleared up with an armed robbery warrant that was on me. In the time I'd been out on bond, I hadn't taken one step towards finding the guy, who placed the phony warrant on me, and try to convince him to drop the charges.

The worst measure yet, was to know that the time I would spend in prison would be ten years to life if I didn't clear up the phony warrant that got me arrested to start with.

I whispered to Britney, "What do they want me for now?"

It really doesn't matter why they want me now. I'm out on $105,000 bond and if I get arrested for anything…anything at all; jay walking, littering or spitting in public, it doesn't matter; my bond will be pulled and when that happens, whatever time I have left to live will be spent behind bars.

Cops don't want to just "talk" to you when they're pounding on your door at three in the morning. I climbed out of bed and slowly moved to look out the back window. It was mid December and a gust of wind blew a light swirl of snow through a stray patch of light in the darkness of the back yard. My bedroom was on the second floor in the rear of the house and since the yard sloped sharply downwards, the distance from the window to the ground was equivalent to a three-story drop. I had no escape that way and since I didn't see anyone covering the back, I figured the cops had figured that much too.

I turned back towards the bed to warn Britney to be quiet. She wasn't there. I moved away from the window and inched towards the bedroom door. Looking down the hallway into the living room I saw four cops draw their guns when Britney pointed down the hallway and said, "He's in the bedroom."

I quickly jumped in bed and pulled the cover up and thought I'd pretend I was asleep. I jumped back out of bed shaking my head saying, "How stupid can I be?"

My next thought was to get dressed since I only had on my underwear. Maybe I'd have time to get dressed before they came crashing through the door.

Why would I get dressed?

I'm a fraction of a second away from the end of my life and I didn't know why I was thinking the way I was thinking. I was in a totally freaked-out panic.

I ducked into the bathroom and just for a moment I was consoled with the idiotic notion that they would go away once they saw I wasn't in the bedroom.

I held my breath and waited until I heard a cop say, "What's that room over there?"

Britney said, "That's the bathroom."

With a heightened degree of panic my fear changed to pure terror. I threw open the window and tried to quietly remove the screen as if not to damage it. Again, I realized how stupid I was acting with each ridiculous decision and just as the cop opened the bathroom door I tore the screen out of my way and dove through the window.

He grabbed me around the ankle and held on to my leg with one hand while pointing his gun at me with the other. He was yelling something I couldn't understand. I was completely outside the window and standing perpendicular to the outside wall of the building. Everything, including the shouting, went into slow motion. It seemed forever that I was caught standing on the outside of the building with nothing but the freezing air holding me up.

I tried to push off the wall but I kicked the officer's hand instead, and he dropped his gun. He loosened his grip on my leg when he tried to pick up his gun and I pulled free and flew away. I floated through space for what seemed to be forever, as each next moment took its time, catching up with me.

Time played a cruel trick on me.

It let me fall so slowly, that I was able to give a great deal of thought to just how bad it was going to hurt when I landed. I didn't brace myself or wince or grit my teeth as I was falling, I just nonchalantly thought of how bad it was going to hurt when I landed and then I accepted the task of waiting for the pain.

I tried to make sense of my feelings, as I floated in mid-air, because I felt as free as a bird in captivity. I was certain that the cops would catch me, but for those exquisitely long moments that I spent sailing through the air, I felt absolutely free.

I analyzed that feeling as I hung motionless in the cold sky. I waited for the ground to rise up, and smash against me, with the comfort to know that if the cops were going to catch me, it would only be a lifeless body that they would have. And, I was Ok with that. Even *that* thought carried with it a certain type of freedom that was comforting to me, and so I waited in midair with no sound, without screaming, and with no bother at all.

I was free!

The huge metal case that housed the air conditioning unit slammed against my face and chest with a force that I thought would kill me. Surprised that it didn't hurt, I lay there and waited for some excruciating pain, but none came. I thought I would feel much worse and so I lay there waiting to feel much worse; and then it came. The *much worse* that came was the two cops that raced around both sides of the house, two cops from each side. Immediately I snapped out of all thoughts of pain or of waiting and I jumped up like a scared rabbit and I ran as fast as I could.

I reached the brush with three cops on my heels.

The fourth cop was faster than the others and was so close to me that he reached out and was grabbing me by the arm when I burst through the first patch of briars. He let go but I kept running through the thick heavy brush. The freezing cold and my panic numbed the pain from the thorns.

I thought of nothing but getting away.

I heard their voices fall further back behind me as I reached the opening on the other side. On this side the thicket opened into what appeared to be a creek. I tried to jump it but only made it half way across. I sunk up to my neck in the middle of a dark thick stench. I heard the cops yelling, "He's stuck in the sewer, quick go around."

My legs churned forward, I clawed, and I grabbed at anything I could find to pull myself up and out, and on to hard ground. As soon as I was out of the sewer, I ran through the back yards of the houses that were on that side of the thick brush and briars. I covered as much ground as I could before looking for a place to hide.

I saw a small open gate two feet off the ground that led to the under crawling of one of the houses, and I dove into it, and pulled the gate closed behind me. There was nothing of any size to get behind under the house and so I crawled to the opposite side of the house and quickly scraped and wormed my way into a shallow impression in the ground. I pulled some plastic sheeting up over to cover me, and I settled in to calm myself and control the noise from my heavy breathing. I lay there perfectly still, and waited in the freezing cold, as I listened to my breathing quiet down.

The cold began to register with me and I lay shivering. I accepted the notion of staying where I was and the thought came to mind of staying right there until summer, if need be; or until a dozen summers passed, it didn't matter to me. My thoughts were that I got away, and now I'm safe. If I had to stay there forever, I would. I preferred the cold and the dirt to another day behind bars.

My heavy breathing settled into a quiet relaxing pace and I felt my body sink into the ground. When I relaxed my neck, my head lowered into the dirt as if it was a soft pillow, and I felt comfortable. In an instant, I felt safe. I closed my eyes in thought of sleep and would have gladly fallen but a sudden noise stiffened my body and shot cold chills through my chest. I gasped a gulp of cold air in, as I jerked my head up off the ground, and I froze in place. My head remained motionless as my eyes searched the darkness. Afraid to breathe, I listened as hard as I could as if my ears could force the sound to show itself. The cold night air was dark and lifeless and was a part of who I was right then. I was absolutely immobile. I couldn't have moved if I wanted to, and so I captured that dark space that I hoped hid me, and I readied myself for what made the sound that frightened me.

Suddenly, the gate leading to the crawlspace, where I hid, flew open.

A beam of light from the cops flashlight washed across the far wall and over the cross beams underneath the floor above my head. The plastic sheeting covered the entire area under the house and the beam of light swept every bit of the plastic including the portion that must have bulged higher than the rest, where I lay. I was certain I was seen to be that bulge when the officer said, "We know you're in here Duke. Come out now while you can. We mean it…come out now."

My thoughts and my heart were racing once again. If I could have moved, I would have run. Even trapped beneath this house I would have run to an opposite corner of the darkness like a dumb frightened animal. But fear paralyzed me and held me in place and I couldn't move.

Did he follow some trail I left? Can he see me? His flashlight swept from corner to corner of this cross basin but the beam of light didn't pause in any direction any longer than another. The portion of the plastic sheet that covered me became so bright the light blinded me, but as quickly as it lit me up beneath the plastic, I turned black again and the beam rushed off in a jerky random pattern.

He doesn't really know I'm here. Or does he?

The gate slammed shut and I heard a piece of metal being placed on the latch that locked the gate. Then the officer spoke again, "This is your last chance Duke, come out. We're going to get the dogs. Come out while you can, the dogs will rip you apart."

There was one last click of metal to metal as the officer secured the lock in some fashion. Before leaving he said, "OK...you had your chance".

Was this really my last chance?

12

I was about to panic but I couldn't find the strength to make a run for it. I was frozen with fear. I felt caught, trapped, suffocated, it was over. They had me. I tried to get my breath back and then, I heard something that made me smile. I let out the air I was holding and melted back into the ground.

I heard the same voice again, and now it came from a distance of a couple houses away, "Duke, we know you're under there, come out now while you can. We're getting the dogs, they'll rip you apart." He paused and then continued, "We know you're in there. You better come out while you can" then the silence returned.

I heard that warning a couple more times. Each time the voice was further away. Each time I smiled and felt better knowing he was just fishing. I dropped my head back on to the dirt.

I thought more clearly now. If I got away, where would I get away to?

Smelling like a sewer and being nearly naked, where would I go all torn-up and bloody at three in the morning? I thought, if I have no place else to go, this must be where I need to be. So I hugged the musty cold earth and prayed the best I could. My prayer brought me peace and I fell asleep.

An alarm clock, from the room above, woke me.

It was light out.

The first thing that crossed my mind was that the cop lied to me. How dare him, he lied. There were no dogs ripping me apart. I lay there and listened to the sounds of the people in the house through the floor above me. I could hear voices and their footsteps as they walked from room to room preparing for their day.

The television was on, a baby was crying, and I heard heavy footsteps that I figured belonged to the man of the house. It was those heavy steps that left first and then I heard a car start up and pull away. Then there were lighter steps, and a child's voice yelling that he was going to miss the school bus, the door slammed shut, and it all became quiet again.

Shortly following the sound of the footsteps exiting, the baby quit crying and the TV quit playing, and there were no more sounds of anyone moving around. There was a rustling sound and occasionally, there was a scraping sound of a chair. There was just enough movement to let me know someone was still there. I figured it to be the mother with her baby.

It was easy to hear the slightest movement from above, and knowing I was just inches below the people above me, I wondered how easy they might be able to hear me. As I slowly pulled back the cold plastic that covered me, clumps of dried dirt made a loud scratching sound, as it rolled across the plastic. Afraid I would be heard, I froze for a second and when I didn't hear anything alarming, I continued moving inch by inch out of my shallow hiding place.

A thousand thoughts raced through my head as I wondered if it was too soon to think I got away. I was alive. I wasn't dreaming; everything that happened to me was real. But here I was…free. I'm not waking up on the metal cot or the concrete floor of a jail cell. Maybe I really did get away. A wide smile cautiously spread across my face and I felt like laughing out loud and shouting, *"There are no dogs"*.

That cop was lying to me.

I did it…I really did it…I got away.

I wanted to run to a telephone and call Marc Crandlemire and tell him that Cobb County's training sucked. "Marc" I wanted to yell to him, "Do you realize that four of your young Cobb County cops couldn't catch an old man like me."

Marc had been the Supervisor of Police Studies at the Georgia Police Academy and had hired me on several occasions to train Law Enforcement Officers. Many times Marc would start the class out with a statement introducing me as their instructor for that week. When I would walk into the room Marc would ask, "How many of you in here have ever arrested this man?"

Immediately a dozen hands went into the air and the room filled with groans.

"Hey, he's not in Law Enforcement," would be the complaint, "What's he doing here, why is *he* teaching us?"

"C'mon Marc", someone yelled, "That ain't right."

"I've been with Clayton County going on 15 years," said an officer, "I've arrested this man six times and I heard that Dekalb, Fayette, Henry, and Fulton counties arrested him that many times as well."

Marc smiled and said, "Yeah, I heard about those arrests."

Another officer started to speak, "Then what…why are you…"

Marc interrupted him and said, "This is your instructor this week. If you feel that anything he teaches you is inappropriate come see me. But for now; that's it gentlemen, have a good day."

When Marc left the room I stood there with a blank face wondering what to do. I've never had so many qualified professionals oppose me like this and right to my face. But there wasn't one shred of doubt in my mind about my qualifications to teach them and teaching them was my main concern, not whether or not they liked me.

I said "C'mon…I'm not much on classroom training. Get your gear and I'll meet you in the gym. You got five minutes to lineup with full workout gear and cartridge belt, holster, and handcuffs."

Now, here I sat remembering those days I taught law enforcement officers how to catch folks like me. It felt somewhat against my nature as an instructor to be glad that they failed. Just the same though, I thanked who ever it was who trained those four guys.

I moved to the small opening that led back out from under the house and into the back yard. A small metal bar was jammed in the latch locking the small gate shut. I pushed my shoulder against it and was surprised how solidly the gate was built. It hardly budged against my shoulder but it made a noise.

About ten feet away and directly in front of the gate sat a huge doghouse. I concluded that some time during my sleep, the owner of the house chained their eighty-pound Rockweiler to a tree on the other side of the doghouse. The noise drew his attention, and he barked once, and then stopped and looked around to see where the noise came from. I sat as still as I could and watched him stand as still as he could. He looked back and forth across the yard but something made him fix his gaze in my direction. He didn't bark because he wasn't sure what this dark figure was that crouched beneath the house, but he watched, and I watched him watch me, and neither of us moved a muscle.

I resigned myself to believe that there wasn't going to be any silent way out of this. I slowly turned myself around until my head was away from the gate, and then I rolled over on my back. I slowly inched myself into position, in front of the small gate, on my back with my knees pulled up to my chest. I took a couple deep breaths and then began kicking the gate repeatedly with both feet. The moment I started kicking the gate, the dog jumped, barked and pulled, and tried his best to get loose from his chain, to get at me.

I kicked the small gate, seven or eight times, and the feeling of doom crept into my chest. For a moment I pictured myself still kicking the gate when the police arrived. I thought what a waste of all this effort. Am I going to get trapped now, after I was so close to getting away?

I kicked harder. I was desperate.

Finally, the gate gave way and delivering two more rapid kicks with both feet the gate fell off at the hinges. I crawled out into the broad day-light, less than a foot from the Rockweiler, who was going mad. Wearing nothing but my underwear, I ran across the yards in the bright morning sun, and made my way through the brush back to my house.

When I reached my house I didn't have the time to make certain the cops were gone. I climbed up the stilted legs of the porch, leading to the back door. I broke the glass, reached in to unlock the door, and quickly stepped inside.

I stood still and listened for any movement in the house. Hearing none, I quickly went from room to room and saw that everything was pretty much the way I left it. My car wasn't in the garage downstairs, Britney was gone, and so was the wad of hundred dollar bills I had in my jeans.

I got dressed on the run as I went through the house checking for things I wanted to take with me. There wasn't anything I cared enough to lug with me back through the woods so I just grabbed my briefcase, check-book, and my phone numbers. My workout bag was under the bed and in it; my Mossberg shotgun and my .44 Bulldog. A wicked smile filled my face as I begin to think of the wild and reckless life to come.

My smile drooped into a regretful frown when I stopped in the hallway to read a letter I framed and hung on the wall. It said that the Secretary's of State from each state in the union were coming to Atlanta for a meeting. The letter said Georgia's Secretary of State, Max Cleland, requested that the Georgia Police Academy *"find the best qualified instructor in defensive tactics in the state of Georgia"* to train a special task force that will be selected to protect the fifty Secretary's of State who were going to be present to attend a special meeting in Atlanta. The letter went on to say that I was the one chosen for that assignment.

When I first started teaching at the Academy there were thirty-eight officers who complained about me teaching them, and as I read this letter that came to me years later, the thought of those disgruntled officers popped into my head.

I remember at the end of the week of that first 40 hour training block I taught at the academy, each officer stood in line to shake my hand and thank me. I never told anyone, but I had to fight hard to hold back the tears as each officer told me what my training meant to them. It touched me that each one of those officers, without exception, gave me the highest mark in every category on the evaluation form.

That day became suddenly blurry, and in that brief moment that I stood staring at the wall, a pain inside my chest told me that I was alienated from these men, that institution, and I would no longer be thought of as I once was.

I took one last look at that letter of commendation from the Secretary of State and said, "I'll be back to get you."

The rush to leave the house slowed to the thoughts of how my life had changed.

I shook it off and finished dressing on the run, grabbed my briefcase and gym bag, and left the same way I came in, out the back, off the porch and through the woods. But this time my life headed in a darker direction.

13

I walked to my bank and cashed a check that would deplete my account. Then I checked into a nearby motel and began making calls. I found Britney. She not only had my car but she had the presence of mind to go through my pockets and find my money as well. Should I have expected anything less of her than to go through my pockets?

As she tells it, "I knew you would get away and you would need your car. And if you didn't get away I knew you would need money to post bond and so I grabbed the wad of cash you had in your jeans and got your car and got out of there."

"OK," I could hardly keep my eyes opened, "Yeah, OK…that's good."

She was pleased to think that I believed her. But the truth of the matter was that if I did get caught I didn't see anything wrong with her watching out after herself. When she was sure that I wasn't upset with her she said, "I knew you'd call. Where are you?"

"I'm on the run baby. I can't believe it…I'm going to have to leave the state as soon as I can. Get over here. I need my car…I got to get out of here."

In her mischievous excitement she asked, "Are you taking me with you?"

Too tired to talk anymore, I whispered, "Come get me baby, I'm at the Hampton Inn…Delk Road…room 317."

I closed my eyes and I was gone.

I dreamt that I was awake, sitting in a deep plush chair next to the bed, and watching myself sleep. I felt as comfortable sitting in the chair, as I did sleeping in the bed. In the chair, I wore dark soft dress slacks, a clean starched and ironed dress shirt, and a light brown sport coat. My hair was short and neatly trimmed, my fingernails were manicured, and I had a rich deep tan from spending too much time with my business buddies on the golf course.

It was hard to believe that the person I was watching on the bed was what I turned out to be. I looked at the long blonde hair that was dirty and matted from sewerage and sweat. That person on the bed, who I couldn't believe was me, wore wrinkled black Levis, a black T-shirt and black running shoes with no socks. The person sleeping on the bed was still wearing a black leather jacket and a black bandanna with skull and cross bone images printed on it. On my hands were black fingerless workout gloves, worn for better handling of the .44 Bulldog snub nose revolver that was in a shoulder holster under the leather jacket. In the workout bag, with my socks and underwear, was my back-up Mossberg 20 gauge shotgun.

Even in my dream, as I watched myself sleep, I couldn't understand how it was that we were so different. We both graduated from the University of California, with a Bachelor of Science in Marketing. We were once the vice president of an advertising agency in Los Angeles, and the national director of a large internationally known martial art organization. At one time we both had been successful in business, as stuntmen, actors, published writers and entrepreneurs. We both were once a respected family man, a father of three children, and even a grandfather.

And now both of us, me and that dirty fellow on the bed, are out of jail on $105,000 bond for armed robbery, and after last night we became fugitives running from the law.

The gap that spans the distance from where I used to be, to where I am now, was once but a small crack in a foundation that I thought would be easily repaired in time. I had every intention on fixing it some day and I never thought that I would let it get so far out of hand.

For me, those cracks started innocently enough as a problem with a relationship. I normally wrote it off as some ridiculous thing the woman in my life was going through. I always saw myself as a victim of their dysfunctional behavior.

Looking at our behavior, the two of me in this dream, it's no wonder the crack didn't get repaired. It got deeper, wider, and eventually I fell in, and got swallowed up. My business associates were traded for 'running mates' and my party life took more of my time than my business did.

The self-doubt that surfaced in my life was that of my manhood. Throw down any gauntlet, and I'd be the one to pick it up, because that was what I thought a man would do. It was my wanting to feel like a man that made me spend so much of my life acting like a boy. I became so obsessed with looking like a man; I couldn't remember if I ever knew what it took to become one.

The pounding on the door startled me, and I jumped up off the bed and fumbled to get my Mossberg out of my gym bag. When I heard Britney's voice I relaxed. It took me a couple more clicks to recall where I was, and why.

When the knowledge of my present circumstances flooded my head I felt a reckless freedom, and an anxious excitement, to begin my new life as a fugitive. As I thought what my life would be like from now on, I visualized a power in me that would no longer answer to, nor be restricted by, the law.

I was sick of the law.

This is the law: Three private detectives drew their guns on me and ran my car off the road. The next day they put a warrant on me and I was arrested. It was explained to me by the detective that he was seeing my girl and he was afraid of me. "It wasn't anything personal," he said "I was building paper on you."

"Paper? What do you mean…paper on me?"

"Well…yeah. You know…I didn't know if we would ever have to face off with each other over Lori. If we did, I could just shoot you…you know, having it on record that you once tried to run me off the…"

"Bull, I didn't try…"

"That doesn't matter. The law has it on record that you did."

The law sucks.

This is the law: A weak little weasel pulled a gun on me and I chased him to his car. He could have gotten one shot off but I would have still been able to do what I told him I would do: "I'll take that gun from you and ram it where the sun don't shine."

He ran.

The next day I was arrested for terroristic threats for saying what I said.

And the law still sucks.

This is the law: The guy living in the apartment in my duplex was sleeping with Britney behind my back. Britney explained it to me that she just couldn't break the habit, "Well at least I don't lie about it do I?"

"Britney, is that where you were?" I could feel the headache that comes when I take to gritting my teeth as she nodded her head. I punched a hole in the wall and yelled, "Why Step, why?

She shrugged her shoulders.

"Damn it, why do you do this to me? Why do you do it and then tell me?"

Her eyes looked at me with a pitiful sorrow in them. Not for what she did but for what she had yet to tell me. "Well, I thought it was better that I tell you."

"Why tell me? Why do it in the first place?"

"I just went over there for a drink. They were playing loud music and…"

"They? Who are…they?"

"Oh Damon had a couple of his friends there, some dope dealers he knows."

"You did them all?"

"I don't know."

"What do you mean you don't know?"

"After a couple drinks I was really feeling dizzy…you know…like when we did that 'H'."

"You mean you were doing HGH with them?"

This angered Britney, "No! I was not doing H with them; they put it in my drink. I know the feeling."

I didn't know what to do. I couldn't go track down everyone Britney saw. Maybe there was no helping her.

"Well Britney, why did you even go over…?"

Then quietly she said, "They were using a video camera."

"What?" I yelled, "Ok that's it." I stood up.

"Don't go, there are three guys, and there are guns lying all over the place."

"Oh that's alright," I picked up my Mossberg and shoved three rounds in and said,"I'll just hold it…won't shoot nobody…unless they shoot first."

I walked across the porch shared by our duplex and Britney stood at our front door and watched me knock on Damon's door.

It was Damon who answered." Yeah? Whatta want?"

"Give me the tape man"

"Hey Ralph…Bo…come here."

Two strung out red necks came into the living room. One of them had a .38 in his belt and when Damon told them what I wanted the other guy reached for a .22 rifle propped up in the corner.

I racked a shell into the chamber and the sound of the shotgun cocking made everyone freeze. Then I held the shotgun by the grip with my right hand. My right arm was down and the shotgun was pointing to the ground. I kept my finger on the trigger

I said, "I don't want any problem. Just give me the tape."

Damon said, "I can't."

The silence was so pure, that the tiny little click my thumb made, when it slid the safety off, gave notice that I didn't feel like playing games.

The guy with the .38 in his belt said, "Oh, go on, give it to him."

"It has my daughter's birthday party on it…I don't want to lose that."

"Just give the tape to me and I'll erase the part with Britney and give it back."

"Ok, I'll bring it over" and he slammed the door.

Five minutes later he did what he said he would do, and brought the tape over to me, and I did what I said I would do. I erased the part with Britney and returned the tape to him and that should have been that.

But three days later Damon hit up on Britney again "Oh come on baby, you guys aren't married. You said you were just roommates."

"Well, he said he was going to marry me and so no more messing around for me."

"What? That old man? You got to be joking."

"No you're the joke Damon. Duke's known about you and me since day one. He said you're just a punk and that you're no threat to him. He's going to get a big laugh at you trying to hit on me again because I tell him everything. He couldn't care less about what you do. He doesn't think it's good for me though, and so he's going to marry me so as I stop. You're nothing in the equation."

Damon's face reddened.

He opened his mouth to say something but Britney spoke first, "So just leave me alone…Ok?"

That afternoon Damon swore out a warrant stating that I put a gun in his face and took a video that belonged to him. He paid the $40 for filing and he had two witnesses backing his story and I was arrested for armed robbery.

The law sets the penalty for armed robbery to be a minimum time of 10 years and can be anything up to life in prison. The assistant district attorney was a woman and she was going over my file with my attorney just a few feet from me. "Normally I would listen to a plea but not on this one. Look at his priors."

"He has no priors. He was never convicted of anything," my attorney argued the point.

"Look at his arrests, assault with a vehicle, terroristic threats, and those are felonies. He got away with those somehow but he won't get off so easy this time. I'm asking the judge to set bail at no less than $100,000. We got him this time." When she shot that glance at me before walking away, I knew it wasn't that I heard something I wasn't supposed to hear…she was talking to me, she wanted me to hear.

The law?

In Georgia, the law sucks.

I was through with the law.

Instead of hanging onto some outer fringe of the law that afforded a thin element of safety, I accepted that there would be no need to walk that tightrope any longer. Why not pull the plug on living safe and let it rip? To hell with the law. Let the chips fall where they may.

I opened the door just wide enough that a body could get through, "Come on…get in here." I took up most of the space in the opening as I stuck my head out the door and looked both ways down the hallway.

As she squeezed by me Britney's mouth dropped open, "Oooh, Duke."

"I'm Ok. What time is it?"

14

My face, legs, shoulders, chest, and arms were covered with a hundred tiny cuts from the briars; my left eye was cut open at the brow and was swollen shut. My chin had a big black bruise right on the point of it and my entire bottom teeth in the front were so loose I wondered how they were staying in.

It was for my leg that I was most concerned. The inside of my right thigh was purple and the skin was torn open just above the ankle.

Britney said, "I thought that cop was going to shoot you."

"The way I feel now, I wish he did."

"You need to go to the hospital."

"No way…they'd be waiting for me."

I made my way back across the room to the bed much slower than it took getting to the door. There was a full-length mirror on the sliding door of the small closet, and I stopped and looked at myself. Now, with Britney there, and my car back in my possession, I no longer saw a torn and battered person worn from injury, exhaustion, and stress. I saw a man in the mirror wearing only his underwear, and a tank top. But he also wore an expression of victory on his face. He lost his 44 Bulldog somewhere and so the shoulder holster was empty but he wore it anyway. It looked cool. The way he held that Mossberg shotgun assured me that I wasn't looking at a defeated man.

I was looking at a man with a mission.

If I ever felt my life was just talk, I didn't feel it now.

"Are you taking me with you?" I could hear the excitement in Britney's voice and her attitude made me mad.

"Britney, this isn't a game. This is real."

That seemed to excite her even more, "I know…isn't that cool?"

"Cool? Are you crazy? I ran from the law Britney. They wanted to arrest me for something and I don't even know why."

"Are you going to take me with you?"

I stopped talking for a second and thought about the life she led.

When we first met, she told me about her first night as a prostitute. It was four o'clock in the morning and she was working the corner of 3rd street and Peachtree in Atlanta. She was fourteen years old.

A man stopped to let her in his car, but when they got to a local park, another man jumped up from his hiding place in the back seat. He held a knife to her throat; they both had their way with her, and then took what money she had before throwing her out of the car.

She walked back to 3rd street and worked the rest of the night, but she never got into another car without looking in the back seat first. That was eleven years and a thousand tricks ago, and now I'm trying to tell her how serious my situation is?

The reason I ran was because, if they caught me, I would spend the rest of my life in prison. That was the reason I ran, but that wasn't the reason they didn't catch me. Something else gave me the strength to get away.

It was because of a promise I made.

In the beginning of my relationship with Britney, I gave her a place to stay and I fed her. I tried to convince her that, if I could see some worth in her, she should be able see it too.

I introduced her to my friends as my roommate, and a very good friend. I wanted to show her that I valued her. I thought if she thought more of herself she would live differently. It seemed to make a change but she kept some of her old, more affluent, customers.

Then, I let everyone know that we were more than roommates, and that we were really living together as a couple. But she continued her profession, "You could throw me out any day and so I need to keep my options open so that I'll always have a place to go."

I only had one more thing to give.

It was around Thanksgiving and I said, "Britney, let's get married."

"You got to be joking." She didn't believe me.

"I'm serious…let's get married."

"That's stupid. Why would you marry someone like me?"

"What do you mean someone *like* you?"

"Yeah…go on…you know what I do. That's all I know how to do and besides there's something I didn't tell you. I didn't finish sixth grade. Did you know that? I didn't finish it. I *went* to sixth grade but I didn't finish."

"So what?"

She paused a thoughtful period of time before saying, "You know…that's right. I could always go back to school. I could get my GED and take up a trade or something."

"Good. You do that if you want. So what about it? Let's get married."

She was quiet for a long moment and then smiled, "Oh man is that weird…me? Married? I never *was* married before." She considered it and then added, "Of course…you know, maybe I couldn't be faithful to a boyfriend, but I could be faithful to a husband."

My head cocked slightly, slowly shook my head, and smiled. She was such a child. I wished there really was something I could do for her, but this was the only thing I could think of. She was softening to the idea of getting married and so I hoped this was what that something was.

"So how do we do that? Don't we have to tell people and make plans and everything?" A fresh idea hit and her face brightened, "Could I get a ring? I got to get a ring, don't I? You got plenty of money, I know…I'm the one who thought to hold on to it for you…but could I?"

I explained it to her, "Of course, we'll get you a ring. We'll go to Ringgold and stop in a store on the way, or something. We can get married all in one day. We can get the blood test, license, and then the JP, all in a few hours."

I stopped to see her response to this.

She calmly searched my face for a telltale sign that I was pulling her leg. I knew the fear that she said followed her into each relationship. It became too quiet for too long, she broke the silence, "But what happens when you don't want me anymore. You'll just throw me out."

"Don't you see?" I said, "Once you are my wife, I can't throw you out. If we argue or get in a fight, you'll have just as much right to tell me to get out, probably more. You won't ever have to worry about not having a place to go. That's really the only thing that I can give you, that's worth anything."

I expected to see more interest from her. I thought this would back up my original motives to help her, the ones that got buried so deeply beneath the newness of this wild way to live.

I got a ray of something back when she asked, "When you want to do it?"

"Oh, I don't know, I'm not sure exactly, but…"

"Oh yeah…*whatever.*"

"Britney…we will. I just don't know when."

"Oh sure. Why did you even bring it up?"

"I mean what I say Britney. I promise…OK?"

Britney walked over and picked up the remote to the TV, "Yeah, sure! Whatever."

She sat on the edge of the bed with her shoulders hunched forward and her head held back, with her chin jutting out and up in the air. She looked down her nose at the TV and started flipping the channels with the remote.

I moved to the bed and sat down next to her. Reaching over and pressing the power button on the remote I said, "Britney, listen…it will be…well, we'll get married…sometime before Christmas…that's a promise."

That was the promise that saved my life.

That was the promise that was in my mind, as a commitment that I would never be able to keep, if I didn't get away from those cops, and that was exactly what I was thinking as I ran.

So now, we made it this far and things looked tough but it was all because of a promise. The bad of it and the good of it…all of it; was in some way connected to this promise.

The quiet space between us brought those thoughts to my mind, and I wondered what that silence brought to her. She stepped forward with the persistence that reminded me of Jack and again she asked, "Are you taking me with you?"

I looked at the lost little girl in Britney's face and I melted, "Of course you're going with me."

"Really?"

"That's right you are." I started to feel the same naïve excitement she was showing. "Look what you did. You took care of my money and you brought me my car. I would be up a creek if it weren't for you. Besides, I promised you that we would get married before Christmas and that's less than two weeks away."

I got up slowly, and said, "So, let's get out of Dodge. I don't feel good here. Any minute some dumb cop is going to pound on the door and I just don't have another chase in me."

She jumped up and was excited again, "My stuff's in the car. Are we going to go back to the house?"

I frowned, "Nah…let's just hit the road."

15

Today was the same day I crawled out from under a house with nothing on but my underwear, and ran home to change my life. I caught a few hours of sleep and then spooked that the cops might show up any minute, I wanted to get as far away as I could and regroup.

It was a bright, sunshiny day.

We must have been a sight as we walked through the motel lobby, checking out just hours after checking in. I cleaned up in the room but that didn't help much in hiding the pain in my face or the areas that wouldn't stop bleeding. I walked at the pace of a ninety year old man moving from his wheelchair to his car, on his way home from the hospital.

It will be a long time coming before I'd be jumping out of any more windows. Anyway, I hoped that wouldn't be necessary for quite a while.

I needed to get my plan in order and catch up with Damon. I had to either convince him that I will not hurt him, for what he had done to my life, or convince him that I will. The latter option would leave no way out for me but that's the way it had to be. I couldn't fathom the thought of dying in prison and never know that Damon died somewhere, just as bad.

I could not get caught until I made one, or the other, happen.

This new role for my life brought a wonderful feeling of liberation. There was nothing anyone could threaten to do to me since I already stood subject to the worst thing I could imagine happening.

At this point I was facing a minimum of ten years to life in prison.

At my age, ten years *was* a lifetime to me. I thought I might as well get something in return for the life I was going to lose. That would be the satisfaction of knowing that the person who took my life, lost his too.

As I drove north to Ringgold I set my mind towards that end.

"Britney, I can't let anything get in my way. I got to see Damon and talk some sense into him before I get caught."

"He's not going to talk to you. He thinks you're going to kill him."

"I really don't want to, but that has to be an option. If I can't get him to drop the charges, that's the way it's got to be."

"Where we going to stop?"

"Where do you want to stop?"

"When are we getting married?"

"How about tomorrow? We can stop in Cartersville now. We're far enough out of Atlanta. Then we can go to Ringgold in the morning, buy a ring for you, get hitched and spend the night in Chattanooga."

Britney scooted over next to me, put her head on my shoulder and in a matter of minutes she was asleep. I drove on past Cartersville with a big smile on my face and didn't stop until we were in Ringgold.

We got up late and drove into the center of Ringgold, Georgia.

When I saw all the cops, I thought surely this idea of getting married was a big mistake. The county offices are where you get the marriage license and the building was crawling with law enforcement. A dozen Squad cars were parked one right next to another and uniformed cops were walking in and out of the buildings.

I freaked out, "Come on Britney, quick back in the car."

"There're not looking for you all the way up here."

"You're probably right…come on, out of the car. Walk fast now. No…no, slow down…don't look suspicious. Hurry…let's get inside."

An afternoon of paranoia got us through the blood test, the purchase of a ring in the only general store in town, and when applying for the marriage license, I thought for sure that by giving my name and information for the marriage license, a dozen cops would barge in to arrest me.

I held my breath at each stage.

It seemed everyone I passed, in uniform or not, looked closely at my banged up face but there was only one comment made about my appearance. The Justice of the Peace said, "Well, you must have put up a good fight, but it looks like she fought you all the way to the altar."

We got married, paid the JP and left.

I couldn't wait to get away from all those cops.

This was not a deep romantic love. It was more along the lines of "God loves you and so do I" and this marriage came about because I had a strong desire to prove to her that she was worth caring for, even after knowing her past. Deep down though, I couldn't imagine anyone being able to see anything worthy in her, and so I saw myself as her salvation and that was the only thing that gave me a feeling of my own self worth.

It was I, who needed saving, but since I couldn't save me; maybe I'd feel better if I thought I could save her. Maybe it was a spiritual investment I thought I was doing. I had no idea why I was doing anything that I was doing, but the bottom line was that I felt, that amidst all the wrong that I was doing, this might be something I was doing that was *right*.

The high point of our "honeymoon" was that we stepped up from the $19.95 a night motels and went right to a motel on a hill that overlooked the industrial part of Chattanooga. This was our 'honeymoon' and so I popped $49.95 for a room for one night. We didn't have a refrigerator or a microwave, but the soda pop machine was only one door away.

Even better, you could walk straight through our narrow room from the front door to a balcony that overlooked the dirty industrial buildings at the bottom of the hill. At night, this valley was saturated with dots of lights extending from the refinery to the railroad tracks that went over the hill to the right. And across this ocean of warehouses, you could see the lights of the houses on the opposite hill from where we were. It looked as if there were hundreds of eyes staring at us through holes punched in a huge black sky.

That was about as romantic as it got.

There were no mushy feelings, but we laughed a lot.

We sat on the dirty orange plastic chairs out on the patio, we smoked a few joints, and she videotaped me acting stupid, and we laughed. We laughed a lot. I forgot all about that crazy person I had become, as I basked in a deep sense of pride that I ran from the law and actually got away. For the first time in my life I enjoyed a feeling of comfort and safety that came from being in control. I could do anything. I was above the law; if they can't catch me they can't punish me. I could do anything.

What I just did though, was to fulfill a promise I fought hard to keep, and that felt good. When I told Britney I would marry her I didn't believe it anymore than she did. It was like I answered a dare with the devil when he said, "Go on and jump from this steeple high above the ground. The angels will protect you…won't they? You won't be hurt."

"Oh; you don't think I'll do it? Because I will, you know…I really will."

The flight seemed peaceful.

After all, what's so scary about falling? Surely, I'll enjoy the wind racing past my face, the breathlessness of free fall, and the weight of the world lifted away. I was overflowing with self centeredness, it was all me. Everything was me, and I was all about filling every corner of my life with what served me. Even the landing will be mine, I don't intend for my family to share my crash. No one else will suffer the fall…will they?

When we couldn't laugh any more we slept, and when we woke, I said, "It's time we get back and see what I can do about all this mess I'm in."

Atlanta was going to be a different place for me now.

As a matter of fact the *world* was going to be a different place, but not for any other reason than the fact that, until I hear 'splat', I was still in it.

16

One day about mid-morning I decided to sneak back into the neighborhood from where I recently escaped. I approached from a direction I never used before.

On the other side of the briars from the backyard I used to call mine, was another back yard. That yard's house faced a street I was never on. I didn't even know the name of that street, but this morning my car sat at the end of that block as I watched for signs of life that might spot me as an intruder. My car idled by the curb as I sat behind the wheel. There was something fresh and free about my place in this morning chill. The street was open for anyone to use but I was held at bay by the fear that the peace I shared with this neighborhood would in any minute be broken.

I was anxious to get this mission started, but I knew there would be no stopping once I started and since I didn't really want to leave this peace I felt, I waited for a good wind of courage to tell me when it was time to go.

This neighborhood stood in a lull that followed the morning clamor of everyone's run at getting into their day. The absence of cars on the street and in the driveways said that people were at work, or away for other reasons. The squawking of an old black crow taking flight halfway down the block broke the silence and emphasized how deeply this neighborhood could fall into silence.

I made my move and drove to the house that I decided to be directly across the briars from mine. I parked and got out of the car in such a natural manner that I would if I were swinging by my house for something I forgot to take with me earlier. I saw myself whistle as I threw my keys a short distance up in the air and catching them after a short hop up on to the curb.

I imagined I might even look like anyone nonchalantly coming by to visit living here. Nothing more, nothing less, nothing wrong with that.

I paid nervous attention to everything around me while keeping my head tilted slightly down so I wouldn't catch the eye of someone looking out a window. I didn't want to face the decision of whether or not to wave at anyone, and if someone saw into my eyes they would clearly see into me. I was afraid they would read too much into my act of belonging there.

I took a deep breath and told myself I had the air of any carefree person stopping by the house in a very normal way. I walked past the first house and then between the next two houses and ducked into their backyard. After taking a quick look to the left and the right and saw that it was clear, I crossed the shallow yard and stepped into the bushes and walked a few steps more before carefully working my way through the briars.

It took me longer than I wanted but I made it to the other side without jumping into any open sewers. I stood just inside the brush behind my house and watched for any activity from inside or down the street. The house was a duplex with two three-bedroom units, one was mine and the other one was Damon's. My purpose was to try and get a hold of some of my things that I didn't want to lose and then to leave Damon a note, a carefully constructed note. No whining or begging but no threatening either.

To the rear of my house any view of me was protected by the wooded area and there were plenty of trees between me and the houses on either side. My back porch was atop four two story high 4x4 stilt-like poles. I crouched by the corner of the back of the house and took one last peek around the corner of the house and down the street before climbing to my porch.

A Cobb County police patrol car slowly turned the corner at the other end of the block and moved towards the house at about 2 or 3 miles an hour before stopping halfway down the block. A black teenage boy ran out to the patrol car just when another patrol car turned the corner and moved alongside the first. The boy was barefoot and shirtless and was not a skinny kid, but he was a kid just the same, and so he was slight in stature and probably weighed 165 lbs. It was the boy who "fell-in-love" with Britney when I was in jail and when I got out he stood in the middle of the street in front of my house and glared at the house as if he were threatening me.

I shook my head and laughed, "Hey Britney, look outside…I think someone's courting you."

The boy leaned down to talk through the car window and pointed towards my house. The second unit put his car in reverse and backed down the street, turned on his flashing lights and without using his siren he raced in the direction of a street I knew to be two blocks away that would lead to the street where I parked my car.

A sudden surge of adrenalin hit me so fast I gasped as I turned to run. My flight was blocked from view by the house and in the light I was able to avoid what cut me up the last time I ran through the briars. How did they know I was there…did someone see me? How long will it take that squad car to get to this other street…were there more cops? Will there be cops waiting at my car?

My heart was pounding so hard I couldn't hear the answers to the thinking in my head. I turned all my focus, in that moment, on getting away. Not until I was in my car and clearly away from that part of town was I able to breathe normal, and in my calm the thoughts poured in.

I still didn't know what they wanted with me, but whatever it was would void my bond, and I would live the rest of my life behind bars. The minimum time for armed robbery was ten years and that doesn't mean you get ten years do five. You get ten years do ten, but they can give you up to life. But even if I only did ten years what kind of life would I have starting over at 67 years old?

The thought of 'starting over' hung with me.

It confused me…this thing; *starting over*. Starting *what* over, going where? Doing exactly what? Isn't it just as bad "starting over" where I am now? Have I started over yet? What do I do in order to begin my "starting over"?

All I know is that I have to stay out here…I have to be free in order to "start over". Maybe I should avoid the word "free" and put in its place, "out here" because I might be out here but I sure don't feel free.

Anyway, no one can take your freedom from you; they can only take your liberty. I know many people out here who have the liberty to go about their day anyway they want, but they're not free. I know people in prison who have no liberties at all, but are as free as they want to be. Right now, I'm just a captive to the thought of being "free".

I had a right to demand that video tape from Damon, and I had a right to protect myself to get it. I was on my own front porch; I never entered his apartment, or pointed my gun at any one of them. I made a request, he brought the tape to me, and I returned it.

In the beginning, I thought the law failed to protect my freedom to do what I did. But the law didn't fail to protect my freedom; I failed to protect my liberty.

A large portion of people in prison today, are there because they believed the same way as I did. I believed I had the freedom to act as I did, but I failed to think what liberties I would give up to be free. We all have the freedom to act as we wish, and when we're locked up, the liberty to exercise those freedoms is what we lose. You can be right, morally and even legally, and still lose your liberty if you don't take the proper action to protect it. I couldn't help but think that maybe the first step of starting over for me would be to get out of Atlanta.

The door was open to our room at the Extended Stay in Norcross and Britney was lying on her stomach watching TV. Without looking up she asked, "How'd it go?"

"Not too good."

"At least you're not in jail."

I froze, "What do you mean?"

"Well, you got away…right?"

"What do you mean 'got away'…how do you know what…"

Britney used the remote to turn the volume up to its maximum and shouted, "What do you mean what do I mean?" and then she started laughing.

I pulled the TV's power plug from the wall. "Damn it Britney I'm not playing. How did you know the cops showed up?"

Her face reddened and just as I thought I read her expression as sincere I detected a slight up turn of the corner of her mouth. The concern in her voice went overboard, "Oh really I didn't know that. What happened? I was just worried about you going over there to start with…that's all…and then you said it didn't go good and now you're back. I just figured…you know…I just figured it."

I stood between the TV and the bed and looked at her for a good thirty seconds or more with neither of us speaking. I took a deep breath and felt my shoulders drop as I exhaled. I wanted so much to believe she was on my side. I finally said, "I'm sorry baby, I guess I'm getting paranoid."

The smile that almost made it to her face fell abruptly into, "Plug the TV in. I'm missing my movie."

I plugged the TV in and lay down on the bed, "We'll wait a couple of days and try again. I have a plan."

Britney didn't answer. She watched her movie about giant ants attacking a space ship on a far away planet and I fell asleep.

Three days later about 4 O'clock in the afternoon we drove to my old house.

Five blocks away I got in the back seat and Britney drove while I hid on the floor. She drove right to my driveway and pulled in and then opened the garage door and pulled the car inside.

The windows on the garage door had been painted black a long time ago. No one could see the car from the outside and so, all we had to do was to keep quiet and not talk in case someone was next door at Damon's. At the far end of my basement, was the room I used as a work area, with drafting boards and a computerized sign machine that cuts letters out of vinyl. I looked through that room and figured the only thing worth taking would be the sign machine. I made a mental note to come back and get it before we left. It cost me a couple grand and it should be worth some money to someone.

I climbed the stairs leading to the door that opened in the upstairs hallway, "C'mon let's get the stuff up here first…the computer, video machine, TV and stuff."

Britney whispered, "I thought you were going to see Damon."

I said, "I am, but first let's get some of my stuff, c'mon" and I climbed the basement steps leading to the upstairs door. "Huh oh, the doors locked," I held out my hand for Britney to give me the keys.

She looked at me and said, "What?"

"Give me the keys...doors locked."

"I don't have the keys."

"What do you mean? Give me the keys."

Britney raised her voice, "I don't have the keys."

A funny silence filled the space between us as we stared at each other.

I said the words slowly in a loud whisper gritting my teeth as I spoke, "Where are the damn keys, Britney?"

With just as much intensity as my question Britney mocked me, "I don't know."

We glared at each other as my nostrils flared and my jaws were set against gritting teeth. We locked eyes and for the next several seconds all you heard was the anger in the breath that stood between us. Suddenly something in her look threw my thinking off balance; I swear I saw a shadow of a smile sweep across her face.

The spell was broke. "Britney, where are...oh, hell with it." I flew down the stairs two at a time and went to the car. There was no buzzing sound when I opened the door. Again, I whispered angrily, "Britney where are the keys?"

"Don't you have them?"

"How could...hey, what's going on here...Britney...what are you doing?"

"What do you mean? Are you getting all paranoid again?"

"That's it. I'm outta here." I threw open the garage door and ran to the back of the house towards the briars. I looked around and then ran back.

"Britney...something's wrong here...are you coming. C'mon Britney...what's going on...did you drop them somewhere? What's happening?"

I felt a strong need to get out of the house...off of that street...away from that neighborhood. I didn't want to leave my car but I was close to panic, I had to leave. I couldn't understand this thing about Britney not wanting to leave with me. I ran back in the garage and looked on the floorboard of the car and in the back seat and under the car. I couldn't find the keys.

I ran back outside, "That's it. I have to go. This has taken too long."

I went out towards the front yard thinking that if I cut through the neighbor's yard to the right of my house I would be one street over without going through the briars. I had to leave and so I stood in the middle of the street, "Britney, are you coming?"

Britney meekly took a step in my direction, anxiously looked up the block and then back at me and stepped back again.

"Britney," I shouted, "Let's go! Now!"

She looked up the street again and appeared to be confused as to what to do.

A thought occurred to me, and I ran in her direction and as I got close to her she stepped back and threw her arms up to protect her head. I ran right past her and to the garage. I flipped the switch on the garage door lock and pulled the door down and it locked shut. I ran back across the street and grabbed Britney by the arm, "C'mon let's go". After two or three steps I was no longer pulling her and she was running alongside of me.

We ran across the neighbor's yard and when we got to the street on the other side behind their house we slowed down and walked. We made it to "The Pub", a small bar five blocks away. We bought a couple of beers and played pool and I tried to think what was going on.

"I got it" the plan came to me after my fourth beer. "I'll call Brian and ask him to…"

Britney interrupted, "Brian? Why Brian…he's such a…"

"Brian's Ok…and he'll think he's doing something dangerous…he likes that."

Brian plays at being bad but he's just a pretty boy dope dealer afraid to go to the south side of town without me.

Britney asked, "But can you trust him?"

"Trust him for what? He's just giving us a ride…who should I call, Scott? He still hasn't brought your sister back. No telling when you'll see her again."

"They were coming back to Happy's…I bet we left too soon…I should of…"

"Look I'll call Brian and he'll get us back to our motel. We can swing by the house first though, and if there are no cops there by now, I'll figure that it was just my paranoia. Maybe then we can stay long enough to look for the keys."

I didn't go into the view I would have if the cops were there.

Forty minutes later Brian picked us up. When we got to my street there was a patrol car in front of the neighbor's house to the right and one in front of the neighbor's house on the left, a patrol car in my driveway and two cars in the middle of the cull de sac were facing my house. There were cops on the porch, in the driveway, on the grass in the front yard and a couple cops looking in the bushes at the rear of the house. What could I have been wanted for, that they would want me this bad? The street I lived on came to an end at my house and if you continued driving you would pull right into my driveway. I was down on the back floor of Brian's Bronco and Britney was crunched down in the front. To turn around at this point would have been a huge mistake.

I wanted to start yelling and let Britney know what I was thinking, because if there were cops there now, it had to be her tipping them off. But if I scared her, or got her mad right now, she may go ahead and give us away. I thought she was going to give us up anyway, but she didn't. She looked just as concerned as I was and kept her head down.

Brian pulled into a driveway half way down the block.

"Hey man, don't turn around now…they'll see that."

Brian said calmly, "I got it covered."

He pulled into the driveway, turned the car off and went up the stairs to the porch. Brian knocked on the door and a young girl answered.

"Hi…is your mother home?"

Just then an old woman appeared behind the girl. She was either the grandmother or a baby sitter. "What do you want?"

"I'm looking for the Ferris family…I thought this was the address. You see he's about 35 or 40 years of age and…" Brian looked down the street and changed subjects, "gee, what's with all the police?"

Gossip was this lady's drug of choice and Brian pulled her into a conversation that brought her out onto the porch. The lady told Brian all about a young girl who was abducted by the older man living at the end of the block. The "old man" was an escaped convict and had ties with the Mafia. Just a couple weeks ago he stabbed the young girl with a butcher knife and carried her body away. They think the body's hid in the house somewhere. "Probably is...you know. The body, probably hid out back, he couldn't be carrying a dead body around with him."

Brian said, "Really?"

The old woman leaned forward and lowered her voice, "I saw her you know. A couple times...she goes to that house over there...where that colored boy lives."

They talked for a decent enough amount of time to make his stopping look legitimate and then he said, "Thanks...I got to be going."

Brian pulled out of the driveway and drove away from the direction of my house and all of the cops. One more squad car came around the corner and passed us in the opposite direction as we turned at the end of the street.

I had held my anger for so long now I wasn't as furious as I was a few minutes ago. Also, the feeling of getting away is awfully soothing to the soul. Instead of ranting or raving I put it in the form of an angry accusing question. "Well, so what do you make of it Britney? Who do you think tipped off the cops this time?"

She surprised me with her response, "You, I guess."

"Me?" I yelled.

"Well, you were the one standing outside your house in the street screaming and carrying on. All those cops showing up; it's exactly what I would expect."

The confidence in my accusatory manner began to falter, "But...but...what about the keys...huh? And why were you so shaky about leaving with me?"

"So I dropped the keys...I was afraid to tell you...you know, having lost the keys...I was just afraid. And about being shaky? I wasn't as shaky as you. Look at what you did. You were standing out in the middle of the street yelling at me, who wouldn't have seen you doing that. Look, Duke, I'm with you and I'm going to be locked up too, because of it."

Oops…must be paranoia?

Paranoia has the look of many things but I still can't buy into this feeling I have about Britney as paranoia. At this time I had no one else and no place to go. No one I could trust. I had to believe this prostitute I've known for only a couple months and then married. My life had fallen to the level of accepting the fact that this was the best person in my life right now. I had to believe her.

Brian took us to our motel and when Britney was in the bathroom I got into my bag in the closet and got a second set of car keys, I told Britney I had to check on a job downtown at the Center Fold, and left with Brian.

Brian drove me back to "The Pub" and left me there. I drank a beer and then walked back to my house. I stayed on the sidewalk to avoid looking like a burglar in the bushes. If anyone saw some dark figure in the night, it would just be a person walking somewhere, but no one would be suspicious, as to where that would be.

I entered my house the same way as before. I climbed the two story stilts to the back porch and went through the kitchen door which was still unlocked. I tiptoed through the house and took a few things that had some emotionally personal value and figured it would be safer to send someone later to gather the rest of the stuff. No one could stop them from gathering my things if anyone heard or saw them here. I opened the door to the basement and started down the stairs.

On about the third or fourth step down, my foot hit something that flew off the stair and hit the basement's concrete floor, making a metallic sounding clang. My garage was underneath Damon's bedroom and so even that little noise freaked me. I ran and opened the garage door and started the car and drove it out into the driveway. I hurried back to close and lock the garage door behind me.

As I ran back towards the garage door I realized I was making good time. This added to my confidence to follow up on a freaky notion. I decided to take the time, and the risk, and I ran to the bottom of the stairs and flipped on the light switch. With my hand stayed on the light switch my eyes hurriedly searched the concrete floor at the bottom of the stairs, and there was the metal that made the clanging sound…my car keys.

I found my keys but that didn't answer the question of how they got there. If Britney dropped them accidentally she would have known she had them to start with and she wouldn't have played dumb and say she thought I had them.

For just a sixth grader, she was really doing a number on me.

17

Britney knew I wouldn't make it through a routine traffic stop, yet all too often I would suddenly realize we were way over the speed limit and when I would tell her to slow down, she would slow down for a minute and then immediately go right back to a speed that could get us pulled over.

One night she came into our room at the Kings Inn and said, "I just saw Cobb County parked outside. They were looking at your car and then I saw men dressed in military camouflage uniforms out back."

I didn't hesitate. I grabbed my gym bag and opened the door and carefully checked out the parking lot and then jumped the banister from the second floor and landed in the parking lot and took off running down the access road to the freeway. I got to the Waffle House on Forest Parkway and tried to call someone to pick me up. I couldn't get a hold of anyone I would trust or who would risk coming around me. I hid in the bushes behind the Waffle House on the side of the freeway for the better part of an hour.

Thinking that something had to give I called the motel and got the front desk, "Listen, I have a friend staying there from out of town and she said there was some kind of military operation going on…something to do with the DEA or Cobb County or something and she's scared…should she be?"

An Indian voice said, "No, no military here. No DEA, no Cobb County…just motel."

"But she said she saw some people in camouflage uniforms out back in the parking lot."

"There is only one. We hire MP's from Ft. McPherson for night watchman. They wear fatigues. Nothing wrong here."

All the way-back to the motel, on the dark access road, I was rehearsing the cussing I was going to pour out on Britney. When I got back to the room I pushed through the door, "Britney, what made you tell me all that stuff about…"

She interrupted me, "Well would you want me to see it and not say anything? Then, if it was what it was, then you'd really be mad."

Maybe I was just upset that she was enjoying this paranoia in me too much but she was right again. I'd rather be safe than sorry.

"Ok, ok," I said reluctantly, "thanks."

"Someone beeped you. A couple people did. You call anyone?"

"Sweetheart, go back by the house and get all my stuff. BB will meet you there and help you. I'll give you a list of things I really don't want to lose."

"What will we do with it?"

"We'll get a storage on the south side."

"Are you setting up any photography jobs?"

"You gotta be joking…I can't work. I need access to my files and I would just die if the cops walked into a school where I was working and arrested me. I have to advertise for a month that I'll be there. I don't think it's too wise to advertise where I'm going to be. I'm on the run, Hon."

"Oh, Ok just asking. What are we going to do?"

"I have some people to talk to. Things will work out."

"You know I can go back to work."

"No! That's exactly what we're trying NOT to do."

"How about dancing then?"

I thought about it, "Hmm…we'll see. Hang in here. I'll be back in the morning."

"Take me to Crazy Horse. Candy will pick me up there."

"Could she pick you up here?"

"I'll call her. If not, I can get a ride."

"You sure?"

"Yep."

"Here take fifty bucks, don't spend it on dope."

Britney put on a devilish air and said, "You know I don't *buy* dope."

"No trades either." I left.

The first game room I went in I was met with, "Hey here's Duke. I bet he can get the money for us."

"Hey Randy whatzup?"

"Oh we're just stewing over some flakes that stiffed us. Hey, I heard how you handled Haney. He's talking real big like he's going to get revenge."

"I thought people said I put the fear of God in him."

"Oh he's just a weasel, gets high once in awhile and talks big. He doesn't mess with Tommy or any of the "rooms" any more. I'll tell you that."

"So how's business?"

"Could be better…you open for an odd job I need done?"

"What is it?"

"We got a guy out in Douglasville. He's in to us for a couple grand. It's really no big thing except that I think he's just letting it die out as though we're going to forget it if he doesn't come back around."

"50—50."

"Fine with us, we just can't let the guy skate on the debt, it's bad for business."

"Just collection though…any more…cost you more."

"Oh that's all, he's alright. He runs a business in Douglasville, doesn't want his wife to know he's gambling so he was coming over this way. But now that he owes us money he quit coming around. We'd like to see him come back. Just collect the money."

"Give me the information on him."

"Listen…you know Michaels?"

"You mean…*Michaels*…*the* Michaels…"

"Yeah. *That* Michaels."

"Haven't met him…heard of him."

"He's got something he needs done and he's looking for someone good. I didn't think you were around anymore…you're always out of town…otherwise I would've mentioned you. I don't know what it is but I get the idea it's pretty heavy. Here's a number give him a call…tell him I gave you the number."

I called Michaels from the car on the way to Douglasville. We didn't talk business, we talked about going out.

"Say, Duke…like the Palace?" He must know I do because he is far above the status of the Crystal Palace. You don't see "high rollers" like Michaels at the Palace unless they get there late, stay 30 minutes at the most, and then leave early, usually with an entourage of women from the Palace and go to a fancy suite downtown or at the airport.

"Yeah…I like the Palace."

"Great. I have a suite at the Best Western near the airport. I have a couple dancers for the night and I'm going to drop them off at the Palace in the morning. How about I meet you there? We'll go have breakfast."

"Sure."

"How's 7 sound?"

"That's perfect."

"See you then and I think we met before. But if you forget what I look like, just look for Benji, he'll be with me and I know he use to work for you. See you in the morning."

That was that.

There was something exciting about taking this step. Michaels was a high rolling dealer that didn't deal with just anyone. He brokered big deals for the biggest dealers and never touches a drug.

It's all money, and all business, with Michaels.

Being the kingpin of the drug trade at such a competitive level is a short lived luxury and so the ones I met in that position lived it to the hilt. They knew the rug would be pulled out from under them any day.

I had time to go to Douglasville and check out the Furniture Store owner that was into Randy for the two grand. But first I called BB. I promised him he could ride with me some time, and since he lives in Douglasville, I thought I could take care of it today.

BB is a pretty boy, a drug dealer and a wannabe bad guy. He's about 5' 11" and weighs about 155 pounds. He's got dark hair and dark eyes and looks as though he stepped out of GQ magazine. He's 25 years old and dates a woman in her forties. Her father is a billionaire and takes good care of his daughter. BB hangs out at clubs on the north side because the ones on the south side are too rough. BB once asked if he could go with me on a collection. Just for the fun of it. He thought it would be exciting.

"Hey BB…can you cut loose…got a job." Then I lied a little bit, if I didn't make it sound real, where was the excitement? What will he have that he could brag about?

So I lied, "Hey I could use some back-up and was hoping you could help me. You know, watch my back."

"Oh really? What is it?"

"Nothing we can't handle, just a collection from a furniture store owner. That's all."

"Can you pick me up?"

"How about 3:30?"

"OK."

BB and I called the store first and found out that our man wasn't at the store so we went by his house. Some people have said I'm a scary guy when I get mad but I don't know about that, I'm too angry to notice. But normally, I'm pretty laid back and I'm just as friendly as anyone lets me be. So when his wife answered the door I felt very much like a door-to-door salesman, overly eager to please and polite. I was surprised at the terror on the ladies face when I asked for her husband. When she left to get him I turned to BB, "Hey, I wonder what's wrong with…damn…BB…lighten up man."

BB was standing with his chest puffed out, his hands balled up into fists, and he had the meanest scowl I've ever seen on his face. It was like he was a stand-in bad guy in a class B movie. I couldn't help but laugh. I wouldn't have been surprised if the lady came back with a gun and shot us both, or else called the cops.

BB was trying to be quite the gangster. I talked to him and got him to lighten up. You'd be surprised at how many of those so called "bad boys" out there are just nine-to-fivers playing the scene. They go home and check their attitude out in the mirror for a while, and then take off their groove and turn into the neighborhood nerd until next Friday and Saturday night which, in my circle, is known as "amateur night".

The Furniture Store owner came out of the house and closed the door and moved to the side where no one inside could see us. He pulled a folded wad of money out of his pocket and thrust at me, "It's all there. I don't want my wife knowing."

"I'm sorry sir but we called the store and they said you went home already. Didn't want to get you in trouble with your wife. But when you're on that side of town, come on by the club. Randy says you're welcome anytime."

We left before we counted the money. I didn't want him to have any trouble with his wife. But it turned out that it was all there. This was so easy. I picked up a grand for myself just for knocking on the door; *this* is what I want to do.

I told BB I had a meeting in the morning but he could ride down to the Palace with me if he wanted.

BB said, "I got some things to do. I'll meet you down there though if you sure you're going to be there. I have three girls that are dying to go to the Crystal Palace. They wouldn't go alone and I told them I knew you and so they wanted to come down and party."

"Ok, I'll meet you there. Here take a hundred for watching my back."

"Thanks man…when can we do it again?"

"I'm working on a deal. Look, I'll see you down there about 5 or 6, my meetings at 7. If I have to leave for a while I'll have time to introduce you to all the bouncers and they'll watch your back. That's our club, man, you'll be alright."

"That's cool."

"Oh yes, could you help Britney get some stuff from my house? I had some trouble; I can't go around there anymore."

"No problem. Just let me know when."

"I'll have Britney call you. We're staying at an Extended Stay downtown."

I dropped BB off and headed back south to hand in the money I collected. I was anxious for Randy to see how quickly it went because I'd like some more of this work, no conflict, no hassle.

Everybody's happy.

18

Randy counted ten one hundred dollar bills and said, "Now why can't my guys do this? It was only a couple grand."

I could have told him but I didn't.

His guys were probably trying to track him down and catch him at another game room and never thought of walking up and knocking on the front door. But that's too easy and I didn't want Randy to know how easy it could be.

"Man, Duke, I bet you put the fear of God in this boy."

"No, nothing like that."

"You're too humble…must be that Martial Art stuff you teach. You didn't want to take the credit for setting Haney on the right track either and now you collect a two month old debt in one day."

"Randy, I'm sort of in a tight…Cobb County primarily…you know?"

"I've heard."

"Just until I get this guy to drop some charges that aren't right."

"Well, if he drops them the State will just pick them up."

"Can't do it. The State would have no one to testify about anything wrong being done if this guy changes his story."

Randy nodded.

"What I need, Randy is a couple more jobs like this to get away from here and get my head together and not have to run hide every time I hear a car door slam outside."

"Tommy was telling me that he tried to hire you to run security on all the clubs. You turned it down."

"Things have changed. Call me if you all still want to talk."

When I got back to the room Britney was gone. She left a note saying she went to her girlfriend's house in Cummings and later she might be at the Palace. I cleaned up and took a nap. She was still gone when I woke up and so I left for the Palace. I left her a note and told her to come on down if she wanted.

I had my own parking spot at the front door. It was mine but I still slipped Preston five bucks for it. As soon as I got out of my car, a car door opened way in the back of the lot and I heard BB call my name across a sea of parked cars. He had three young women with him and introduced them to me. It was the most amazing thing I ever saw, each one was more beautiful than the other until you looked back at the other and then she was the one more beautiful until you looked back at the next, etc.

What a life to be twenty-four years old, a GQ pretty boy, a drug dealer, and to have a friend like me, and then, to be at the Palace on Saturday night.

I couldn't believe the girls BB had with him. There was Jennifer, Christina, and Amanda. You could tell they were used to being around money by the clothes and the jewelry, but more than anything else, by how out of place they looked to be at the Palace.

I didn't want these thoroughbreds to have to jump the chain. I pounded on the back door and Scott, the bouncer I met the last time I saw Kiwi at the Palace, opened the door and we gave each other a high-five and I said, "They're with me" and we all went in.

You could tell these young ladies were in the habit of being taken care of. They entered with an air of owning where they walked, as if very place they set their foot was theirs. They chose a place at the back bar and, with teeny little steps, crowded in between two tall barstools, hugged each other and like three little kittens huddled between the two barstools with me on one stool and BB on the other.

Pretty boy and Mr. Bad flanking three gorgeous flowers that gently held on to each other and more firmly on to us. Amanda in the middle was holding on to Jennifer's arm and laced fingers with Christina whose right arm rested on BB's back, her hand softly caressing the back of his neck. Jennifer's left arm was leaning on my leg with her left hand absently stroking the inside of my thigh. Our backs were to the bar so that we could watch the club vibrate to the music. The dance floor was two levels. The dancers who thought they were the hottest danced on the upper stage in front of the mirror. The dance floor itself was a hard translucent Plexiglas with colored lights underneath. The lights changed colors to the beat of the music as did the walls, tables, faces, and chairs.

Everything vibrated to the beat of the bass of the music but the women in their short skirts vibrated to more than the music and the skirts inched their way to the tops of their thighs.

If I tried to stay cool and not move, the urge to join the others gripped me. But tonight I followed BB's lead and it took all I could do to sit still and play the macho action as the girls between us moved with the music. Their body's danced in place while BB and I sat frozen, looking out over the dancing heads across the club. I saw people I knew look in our direction and point as though we were quite the "in" sight. I sat as tall as any king would do and returned their wave with an approving smile and a slight nod of my head.

Our trio was dancing more vigorously now. Their hands were all over each other, and more so, all over BB and me as their bodies danced and brushed gently against us. If I were less a man I would have hoped Kiwi could see me then, but with action like this I can gladly say no thought of her entered the world I was sharing with Jennifer, Christina, and Amanda. This was my moment, and little did I know it, but BB was about to turn up the heat.

I asked "What will you have girls?"

They all turned to BB and smiled and continued dancing. They each looked at me at separate times and gave a quick smile and shook their head, looked down in their dance and turned away, and then back again. I wasn't sure what was going on but it was Ok with me. Everything was Ok.

BB turned to Brian, who was bartending, and yelled above the music, "Bottled water?"

Brian nodded yes.

"Give me five…keep the change" and left a ten and a twenty on the bar.

"Let's move," I pointed to a table that just emptied.

On the way over I said, "Hey BB…how do you do it, man?"

"It's easy; you just have to have what they want. Here, watch what happens. I'm going to tell them you're *the man*. You know? *My* dealer. Where I get my stuff."

"No man, don't do that. I don't have anything on me. Maybe, half an eight at the most."

"Forget that." BB dumped a handful of Ecstasy in my hand. "Here take this."

It was literally, a full handful. I was dropping them as I rushed to jam them in my pocket.

Now the bottled water made sense and the fact that they couldn't stop moving so fluidly. They were on X and as BB said, "In a minute Duke, you'll be *De Man*."

BB moved closer and spoke directly into my ear, "When you see one of them coming over to you put a tab on your tongue but don't swallow it. Remember how Cathy would pass you the X…remember? Put one on your tongue and then sit down and wait. Each one of these girls is going to want to come up and kiss you, so be ready."

I watched BB talking to the girls. Then I put a tab on my tongue and Amanda stood up, the music was loud and she danced over to where I was sitting. She danced in front of me and then hiked her dress up and straddled me. She put her arms around my neck and I felt her dancing in my lap. As I looked up at her she opened her mouth and placed a warm wet kiss on my mouth. Her tongue was sweet and I felt it reaching for the tab and so I pushed it into her mouth and she closed her lips and took the tab. With legs spread wide she stood up and leaned back as she drank her bottled water. She bent so far back that, if I didn't have my hands wrapped around her tiny waist, she would have fallen.

When she was through drinking, she collapsed into my lap dramatically, and draped loosely across my chest like a rag doll. She stayed there for a moment or two. Her head was on my shoulder and when she raised it, her cheek rubbed against mine and her lips brushed against my ear, as she said in a loud whisper, "You are soooo good."

Then Jennifer followed with much the same routine and then there was Christina. After they all got their kiss of X they danced. They brushed every good part of their body against us as they danced. BB and I sat and talked about wild and dangerous stuff like it was big business. Most of it was made up or exaggerated but we carried on so that the girls could hear us being big shots.

Their dancing rubbed against us as they tried to get our attention. They had every bit of my attention but BB told me that the game was to not let them know they were driving me up the wall, "Be cool," he said. "That drives them up the wall and they just try that much harder."

For about an hour or so, BB let me be *the man*.

Now, I know why dealers do the things they do. An hour passed too fast for me, and before the girls wanted anything else from me, I saw Benji standing by the front door. He was talking to a stranger.

It was time to get back to the world I knew best.

19

Benji motioned for me to meet them outside.

Michaels looked like who I thought he would be but I couldn't remember where we met. I followed them over to the Best Western and we talked briefly about the women we knew.

It seemed to interest him to tell me that he sees Kiwi from time to time. I asked him, "What are you trying to say to me?"

He took a quick look at Benji, "Hey man, why don't you go do that thing you need to do...see you back in about an hour."

After Benji left, Michaels said, "I'm seeing her now and I wanted you to know that. I wanted to make sure that wouldn't be a problem."

"Kiwi? A problem?"

Michaels smiled and looked directly into my eyes as if waiting for something more from me. I added, "If you're seeing Kiwi, more power to you, join the crowd. I'm not seeing her anymore."

"No Duke. That isn't it."

"Really...Kiwi and I are..."

"It's not about Kiwi and you."

"Then what?"

"It's San Ji."

I shrugged, "What about him?"

"San Ji's got some problems...business problems." Michaels got up and went to the refrigerator and pulled out a carton of cranberry juice and held it up towards me with an empty glass in his hand. The inquisitive eyebrows completed the question.

I nodded.

He poured.

"This is awkward Duke. I have a problem with San Ji and it doesn't have anything to do with Kiwi. But because she's in the picture it's going to look like she's the problem, and although she isn't, I have to be light-years removed from anything that happens."

"Happens? So what is it you got going with San Ji?"

Michaels shrugged, "San Ji needs to be dealt with, that's all." He handed me the glass of juice. He drank his juice and placed his glass on the counter near the sink. He stared at the empty glass as if contemplating something.

As soon as he started to talk again, I stood up and interrupted, "Hey man, I need to use your bathroom." I walked quickly past the bathroom door that was clearly visible, and near the kitchen, next to where Michael's was sitting.

Instead of the bathroom door, I opened the bedroom door, "Bathroom in here?"

"It's right there." He pointed to the bathroom I just walked past.

I ignored to where he was pointing and said, "Oh I see it." I went through the door and went into the bathroom in the bedroom. I didn't use it but I turned on the light and came back out and as I walked by the bed I laughed and jokingly pulled up the bedspread and looked under the bed, "You're not hiding any cops in here are you?"

He knew what I was doing and he didn't take offense to it.

The room was clean.

I asked, "So what's the deal?"

Michaels said, "Nothing to it. San Ji needs to get hurt. It's going to happen. I just thought you might want to be the one to do it."

"Kiwi's nothing to me. That's all over with."

"Ok, then she's nothing to you, I'll buy that. But that's not why I'm talking with you. It's just because you're the right man for the job."

This in-length talk of "the job" was starting to unnerve me. "What exactly do you mean when you say 'job'? I mean how bad do you want him hurt, exactly?"

"Not bad really, but when he wakes up, I want him looking at heaven."

There was a lot to consider.

Do I accept the job and do it, or do I accept the job and do Michaels? Do I accept the job and warn San Ji and let him get away, or do I argue the merits of San Ji and try to change Michaels's mind, or do I look like an nine-to-fiver and say, "No, I don't do things like that"?

There were a number of ways to go at this. I decided that the best thing to do is to accept the job and then see what happens down the line.

I asked "How much?"

Michaels said, "It's your job you tell me."

"$1500."

Michaels agreed, "OK, five hundred now and…"

I cut Michaels short with what I thought would be a deal breaker, "Oh no, all of it now. I won't be reachable after the job and chances are, neither will you."

Michaels smiled as he opened up a brief case and counted out fifteen one hundred dollar bills from a stack that told me I could have charged a lot more. He laid it on the table in front of us. Then Michaels took out an odd looking brown cloth glove. It was the oversize brown cloth glove you would wear when working in the garden. He said, "I have something for you" and laid it in front of me.

It made a muffled clunk when he put it on the table.

I looked at Michaels and he nodded to the glove and I picked it up. It was heavier than a glove would be and there was a hard metal object in it that was easily discernible to be a gun. The cloth glove was loose around the gun and there would be no problem cocking the hammer or pulling the trigger with the gun being inside the glove. The opening of the glove was wrapped shut with duct tape.

Michaels said, "It's clean…no prints…no serial number. It's only a thirty eight so one shot won't get it. You know as well as I, a single thirty eight round won't do much damage, so double tap him or get up close to begin with. You know your business."

I noticed his language and wondered what police training he had gone through. I didn't think he had a background in law enforcement. The term to "double tap" is what I taught at the Police Academy, which meant that instead of going for the smaller target like the head, your first shot hits center mass (chest) and immobilizes the subject for an instant, making the second shot easier to make to the head.

There was a rumor going around that I dismissed before now. The talk was that Michaels was in with the four cops suspected of busting safes out of the walls of several night clubs in Atlanta. They would take them to Jackson Lake and after breaking into them, they tossed them in the lake. Two of the cops shared a cabin at the lake. Someone "dropped a dime" on them and they dragged the lake and about a dozen empty safes were pulled up, all in one area. Four cops were put on leave pending investigation and more arrests were to follow. No one said who "dropped the dime".

The word on the street was that "someone" was rolling on his drug connections, and these guys just accidentally got caught on tape, saying the wrong thing at the wrong time.

As these thoughts swarmed back into my head I unconsciously reached my hand up and touched the crystal, yin yang medallion, and the feather lying on my chest.

I hadn't said anything yet.

He continued on pitching his side, "When the job is done pull this tape off and let the gun fall. Don't drop the glove or the tape anywhere near the scene. It's easy as that."

I picked up the glove and gun and put it in my coat pocket. I reached for the money and Michaels said, "Then we got a deal?"

"Yeah, we got a deal."

"Looking at heaven?"

Like a stranger listening to someone else talking, I heard my own voice say, "Yeah…looking at heaven."

As soon as I left Michaels I blocked out what I just got paid to do.

All I thought about on the way back to my room was how I could get to Damon without scaring him. I knew I was going to get caught soon and I couldn't have that armed robbery charge on me when that happens.

Britney wasn't in the room when I got there and as soon as I closed the door I was suddenly exhausted. The need to grit my teeth and tighten every muscle and stay totally alert fell off me as the door closed and locked behind me. I was exhausted from the day's activities in my new world but sleep…*restoreth my soul.*

Each time I wake up I am given another chance to choose what direction to go. But today I didn't feel the choice was mine anymore. Another heavy commitment and the thought of freedom slipped further away.

When I woke up Britney was sleeping next to me. I shook her gently and said, "Hey baby. You awake?"

"Damn you Duke," she pulled her shoulder away. "I was…"

"Good, I need to talk to you."

"What time is it?"

"It's 8 O'clock."

"No it's not. It's still dark out."

"It's 8 baby, it's night, c'mon get up and let's grab a bite to eat. I'm hungry." I rummaged through my bag of clothes and found some clean ones and jumped in the shower.

I was talking as I opened the bathroom door, "Britney, we need to find Damon. I got to work on having this charge on me dropped."

"What's the hurry?" Britney was sitting Indian style on the bed as she watched cartoons on TV and ate a peanut butter sandwich.

"Hurry?"

"Yeah, you got plenty of time. And we're having fun, ain't we?"

"Britney, lower the volume?"

"Hell no."

"Britney; just for a minute. I want to talk to you."

"I'm watching TV."

"It's cartoons Britney, it's cartoons"

"So what? I'm watching it."

"Britney this is serious, turn it down and listen up."

"I said, NO."

I reached over and grabbed for the remote but she grabbed it too. We wrestled for it and I had to twist her arm and yank it out of her hand. I turned the TV off.

Britney was cussing at me under her breath as she reached for the phone on the nightstand. When she was connected to an outside line she dialed 911.

I asked, "What are you doing?" I waited to see what she would do.

She started speaking, "There's someone here you want…"

I snatched the phone out of her hand and put the receiver to my ear. There was a 911 operator talking, "What is your location? Do you need medical attention?" I slammed the phone down but I knew it would only be a matter of minutes before they would have the number traced and a squad car would be pulling up.

I yelled at Britney but I didn't have time to do what I really wanted to do to her. I didn't want to strangle her. I didn't want to hit her or shoot her. I just wanted to stand in front of her and yell at the top of my lungs and scream and cuss and beat my head against the wall.

But I didn't have time to do all that. I had to finish getting dressed and then run from the closet to the bathroom and back to the dresser gathering up everything that was mine. I made a mad dash out of the room and threw it all in the car and jumped in. I was backing the car out when all of a sudden Britney came running around the corner yelling, "Wait…wait…I'm coming with you." She had the black garbage bag with her clothes and personal belongings in one hand and her curlers and a can of hairspray and an over night bag under her other arm.

I leaned over and opened the door and she threw everything she was carrying in the back seat, got in, and slammed the door, and with a big grin on her face, said "Let's hit it."

I drove away on whatever road my car found first, before finding a freeway. We stopped at a place to the north of Atlanta that was close to where I used to live and to where Damon was still living. We checked into a Days Inn and unloaded the car and then parked it around back, out of site.

While Britney was in the bathroom I hid the remote control under the mattress of the second bed. Now, I finally had time to stand and yell and cuss and bang my head against the wall but I was too exhausted.

Instead, without a word, we fell asleep.

20

I never thought this was the way my life would turn out. I never thought it was possible for anyone to get lost in plain sight the way I did. I'm nothing to anyone passing by, no one can see me. Not even those eyes that are always watching me, they don't see me either. I don't know what it is they see, but it isn't me.

I'm invisible.

I'm on the run.

I'm hiding.

I'm nothing.

I'm nowhere.

I can't be seen.

Whether I'm sitting in the darkest corner of Club Anytime at four in the morning or at McDonalds at four in the afternoon, I lower my head and study the dark lines burrowing into my weather worn hands and disappear into the music that comes from the ringing in my ears. When I'm tired I lay out a line of speed on any table in front of me and take it in and I wake up. That was alright for me to do because, unless I looked at you, you didn't see me.

All I wanted was a family but when I got one, I lost it. I knew nothing of how a 'family' was supposed to be. I wanted to be loved and never once did it occur to me to genuinely love in return. I didn't know how to accept love any better than I knew how to give it and so I searched harder for the love I could have, than for the love I could give, and in the process, I weighed myself down with good reasons not be loved.

Even when I was aware of what I was doing that drove people away I searched for ways to be forgiven rather than for ways to not drive them away. When I met Britney though, I was drawn to someone who I thought needed love and forgiveness more than anyone I ever met, and that made me think that if I could love Britney, I would earn the right to be loved by anyone. I found out that people don't necessarily *want* something just because they need it. And even if they want it, it doesn't mean they want it from me.

Britney and I never had a place that we called home since we left the one I had when we met. We traveled from one motel to the other and living on the street became our home.

We knew where the drugs were being cut on Thursday to get ready for business on Friday, but so did the drug dealers who didn't have the money to buy their own. The result was, a few dealers would rob other dealers and take their stash, and no one could call the cops.

But they could call me.

Britney and I would have a place to crash a few days a week because I was paid to protect one group until they hit the street and then I was paid to recover what another gang stole from someone else who I wasn't protecting when they were robbed.

This way of life was quite different than how I thought I'd live, but for some reason I thought I could get used to it. I figured I could handle it just until I got the "armed robbery" charge off my neck, then I'd get right.

The cops were still looking for me but I didn't think it was like it was before. The best time to travel, and tend to business, was during the day. One lone car on an empty road at four in the morning sticks out a bit much. The percentage of police vehicles in traffic increases sharply with how late it is. Therefore, when you see a car late at night the chances are too good that it's a cop.

It was six o'clock and Damon would be home from work and I needed to talk with him. "Britney, we're going to the house. We'll drive separate cars. You take my Subaru, I'll drive the Saab. Since I rarely drive it I should be less noticeable. You knock on Damon's door and I'm going to be down the street and watch the house. If he let's me, I might be able to buy him off."

"Buy him off? What you got baby...you holding out on me?"

"I got a job babe...just leave it alone, I got a job."

She gave me a sideways look and I could see she sensed there was something new in the way I talked to her. She didn't push it but, in a slow guarded delivery she asked, "Ok...but what am I going to say...to Damon?" She eyed me with suspicion.

"Tell him I want to talk with him."

"Oh no, I'm not setting him up for *that*...I'm not getting involved with *that*."

She saw too much. She saw something I didn't think she'd see but it was there, the moment I accepted the $1500 from Michaels there was a part of me I never saw before either, but it was there, and now Britney seemed to sense it, too.

I took payment to kill someone and although I didn't see myself really doing the job, I was a different person for saying I would. The thought of killing someone seemed to be such a long way off from my reality but, in a strange and dangerous way it made me feel important and if I was going to kill one person, why not another?

I closed my eyes and tightened my lips and shook my head in a few quick short shakes. I waved off that part of me that Britney was sensing. "No, no, no, I'm not going to hurt him. I just want to talk to him."

"He's not going to talk to you."

"Ask him. Ask if he'll talk to me on the phone?"

"He doesn't have a phone."

"I know baby," I pointed to her cell, "but you do. Call my number and give him the phone."

I looked straight ahead but I felt her staring at me, "When are we going to go to North Georgia. We are going aren't we?"

"Yes baby, as soon as I get out of this mess."

She followed me in the Subaru to our old neighborhood and I motioned to her to hold off a block away and wait. I pulled around the corner of my street a good block away from the house and parked my Saab at the end of the block with a clear view of Damon's front porch at the end of the street. I dialed Britney's cell phone and she answered. I said, "C'mon" and hung up.

A minute later Britney turned the corner and passed me in my Subaru. She drove down the block as planned and pulled into Damon's driveway. She got Damon to come out and talk on the front porch and I was holding my breath. They talked on the front porch for about five minutes and I finally got a break. My phone rang and I saw it was Britney calling and I could see her handing the phone to Damon.

It had been a long time since I heard Damon's voice. But the minute he spoke I recalled that Damon wasn't really all that bad of a guy. In the first minute of our conversation he conceded that none of this problem would have happened if it wasn't for Britney.

I wanted more than ever now to talk to him in private. I sensed that he wouldn't talk freely in front of Britney and since I needed to convince him that this whole mess wasn't between him and me, I had to be free to place it where it belonged; on Britney.

But I didn't want Britney to get mad and sabotage my progress.

Damon was sitting on the top stair of the staircase leading to the front porch. Britney was seated halfway down the stairs. I could see them in the distance from where I sat in my Saab.

I chanced it, "Damon, how about if I come over. I'm really not all that far away."

Damon jumped up from where he sat, "Don't you come around here…I mean it. I'll call the cops." He moved across the porch and stood in front of his door and looked around to see what I meant by being close by.

"No. I wouldn't come by unless you said I could. I was in North Georgia for a while…now that I'm back in Atlanta…I just thought that…you know, maybe we could get…"

"No way man…you're crazy."

"Damon, I've had three months now and at any time I could have killed you. I'm not going to hurt you. You should see that by now."

"I don't care. You both are crazy and you freak me out."

I heard Britney in the background, "Kiss my ass, Damon."

This is what I was afraid of, Britney just couldn't keep her nose out of things, "Hey Damon…Damon…stop a minute. Give Britney the phone a minute."

I could see him walk across the porch and hand Britney the phone, I said "Britney, do me a favor…a BIG favor…go to Qwik-Pic…get yourself some cigarettes…buy a Coca-cola…buy some ice cream…buy a Lotto ticket or two…read some magazines. Go do *something*…anything, but I don't need you aggravating this guy right now. This is the closest I've ever been…come back in…in…fifteen minutes or so…OK?"

She gave the phone back to Damon. I could see from where I was that she was in a huff but she handed over the phone and left.

"Damon, do you want this nightmare out of your life…I mean like it never happened? You want to see us disappear?"

He waited for more.

"Then tell the court what really happened…"

The Subaru was coming towards me from that end of the street and just as it passed me, Britney stuck her hand out the window high in the air, her middle finger was extended and pointing to the sky.

I tried to keep cool and not break my sentence, "drop the charges. Help me out here Damon…you know this wasn't my fault…and I know it wasn't yours. It was all Britney's doings."

"You don't know the half of it."

I sensed more was coming and so I shut up and let Damon continue on his own.

He started out by telling me how terrible it was for me, a man my age, to be living with and then marrying a twenty-five year old. I listened to his accounts of how he heard how we fought all the time and how he was interested in helping Britney only because she was asking him for help to get away from me.

"Oh, really?" I raised an eyebrow and listened.

"Who do you think called the cops every time you came around…it wasn't me, it was that black boy she's been seeing down the street, Marcus."

"Oh she told me he was infatuated with her once…that's all that…"

Damon laughed, "You are really a fool aren't you? She didn't quit coming to see me because of you. She quit coming to see me because she's been seeing Marcus. All she ever talks about is Marcus. Come on man, don't you even know why you're running?"

"What do you mean…what would you know about…what do you mean?"

"Do you remember that day you got drunk and broke the glass table in your kitchen? That was the night they pounded on your door and you jumped out the window and ran."

"What about it?"

"You were mad about something and you left the house and didn't come back until later that night."

"I had business…it wasn't anything to…"

"The cops came that day and Britney had a scratch on her arm and she said you tried to cut her with a knife."

"It was an accident. She swung at me while I was in the kitchen cooking. She swung at me…"

"But I heard you all fighting after that and that's what I told the cops."

"We weren't fighting. I was trying to shut her up. She was mad at me because I told her to leave. I was cutting an onion and she swung at me. I pulled the knife back away from her but when it scratched her hand she looked at the scratch and then smiled, and in a deliberate and cold tone she yelled at me *'I got you now'* and then she started screaming her head off. It was just an act. She ran out the door screaming and I pulled her back in and tried to get her to shut up. We fell on the floor and I was trying to put my hand over her mouth and I kept begging her to shut up. I got her quieted down. She knew it was a mistake that scratched her arm. She knew it."

Damon said, "Maybe so, but when you left, she walked up to Marcus's house and thirty minutes later the cops came. She told Marcus that you tried to kill her and he called the cops and she swore out the warrant."

I couldn't say anything. I was in shock.

"It's her and Marcus, he's in love and she…what can I say? She still comes over here to see him."

I shook my head, "But…but, he's only 17 years old."

Damon laughed, "Britney is only 25 and how old are you? Fifty-five, fifty-six, fifty-seven frigging years old…man, are you that dumb?"

"But I was trying to help her get her…why would she be trying to get me put away?"

I almost heard compassion in Damon's voice, "When you weren't married she was just going to steal all your stuff but you got out on bond. But before you got out on bond, Marcus was living there…in your house…with her, while you were in jail. He would bring 2 or 3 of his friends over and they all would be running around the house naked."

"You saw this?"

"Oh yeah, I went by one night and they were all naked and she was on the floor dropping hot wax on herself…"

"Where?"

"Where do you think? Where it felt the best…she was showing off for the boys. They were all naked."

I argued the point, "But she doesn't have to steal anything…"

"You're right. She has all your stuff now…it's you she doesn't want. If you're arrested she gets your stuff without you. To her, that's a lot of *stuff*."

I was quiet.

It all seemed to fall in place.

A question played back in my mind about the night the cops came, "Why did she open the door?" The image was there of her standing in the living room pointing down the hall, "He's in the bedroom." I thought she was just too scared not to open the door but if she was scared she would have asked me what to do. She would have looked to me but now that I know her better, I know she's not afraid of any cops pounding on the door. She's been around…seen that, done that, got the T-shirt.

All those times she would go over the speed limit when she was driving, she was trying to get a cop to stop us, not for the ticket but so the cops would get me. The cops were always showing up at times that they would have no other way of knowing that I would be there, especially when I went to the house. There were those times she called 911 and pretended it was a joke, and then there were all the times she created a scene, at a weird time, in public.

It all seemed to fall in place but I didn't want to believe it. "Then why doesn't she just call the cops and turn me in."

"She wants you out of the way but don't you realize how scared people are of you? She doesn't want you to know whose pulling the strings until she's sure the plug on you is pulled for good. She was surprised you got out of jail the last time."

"You mean you all planned that?"

"No, I really thought I was helping her because she said she was afraid to leave you. She was playing you and me against each other. She was probably lying about me as much as she was bad mouthing you. She's a snake and I don't know what to tell you man." He laughed, "You're the one who married her. I want her away from me and I want you away from me, both of you are nuts."

"I know how to get that done."

"How?"

"Tell the D.A. the truth."

"How do I know you won't…?"

"Damn it Damon, the way you know I won't do anything is because I haven't done anything, and when this is cleared up I won't have a reason to do anything. If I'm such a bad guy I would do something now while a reason exists and I don't, so why would I do anything when a reason doesn't exist?"

Telling him what I could do to him must have challenged him in a distant sort of way. It's like when two men yell at each other on the phone in a way that they wouldn't yell at each other if the distance wasn't between them.

They go on threatening each other for a while until they both escalate into screaming and challenging each other while a safe distance away. But neither makes the effort to go to the other and do what they say they could do.

So, I guess I challenged him in this way because he said, "So you think you're really bad huh?"

I needed to shorten the distance before we got into one of those ridiculous across town telephone-safe yelling matches, "Damon, I'm not saying I am bad. I'm just saying that there were times I had the opportunity, that's all."

"Oh really, aren't you the tough guy?"

Oh no! He was starting that distant "bad guy" crap. People are so brave when they're on the phone.

His cowardly bravado touched a sore spot and my ego got the better of me, and even while I was talking I knew I was blowing the whole deal. My ego just got the best of me.

I came unglued and yelled, "Yes, Damon, it wouldn't take anything for me to run up those stairs and take that silly looking Braves ball cap off your head and shove it where the sun don't shine."

Damon had earlier sat back down on the first step and now he jumped up again.

"Don't jump up, stay seated. Let's talk about the word *opportunity* Damon."

I was blowing it. I was just so tired of talking to this jerk.

Damon looked around nervously in quick jerky head movements, "Where…where are you…what are you doing?" He slowly walked back towards his front door.

"Don't leave Damon. Stick around, I'm just asking for your help."

"Why? Why should I…you give one good reason why I should." He continued walking towards his door.

"I John 3: 11."

"What?"

"That's my one good reason."

"So what is John 3?"

"No…it's *first* John three, eleven. If nothing else will do it, then consider that."

"I don't get it…what do you mean?"

Now I wished I hadn't shown him my underside. I didn't want to soften in front of him. It was killing me to let him have this upper hand. Even the way he asks his questions is demeaning and snide. The one thing I did not want to do was to get personal. I much rather just smash his face into a concrete wall and go to prison and be done with it.

That was all I wanted to do but I grit my teeth and fought that image out of my head and said, "Look here Damon, what do I have to do?" I paused and took a breath. "The past few months I've been on the loose, have I done anything to cause you a problem? I could have, and what would you do about it? Call the police? They're already after me, stupid. Now, you stop and think about it, the warrant you placed on me was a lie and anything I do to you would be morally right to me. But I know Britney was the problem, not you. You must know Britney is your problem, not me. I don't know what else to do. If you just want *me* to be your problem you are making the biggest mistake of your life. You know that was a phony warrant, they call it an "abusive warrant"…and it's going away…or you are." I listened to myself trying to reason with him and got angrier by the second. "How dare you think you are going to continue to mess with me and get away with it. I'm tired of it, man, I'm tired of it…if my life is over, it will be for something real, not because of a crappy lie from a weasel. So Damon, you do what you want, I'm over it. Leave the phone on the porch. Britney will pick it up, I've been here too long…I'm gone."

"But how can I be sure that…"

"It's over Damon…it is over. I know where you live. I know what you drive.

I know where you work. I even know where you park and what street you take to get home. It is over. You do what you want and I'll do what I want."

"Wait…wait, what if I…?"

The phone went dead as Damon watched a silver Saab at the end of the street move from the curb in reverse, back around the corner, and then drive off in the direction of Qwik Pic.

21

I saw Britney and my Subaru coming towards me, on her way back from the convenience store. We stopped in the street facing in opposite directions. I rolled down the window and we talked across the white line. It was a neighborhood street. We had a minute or two.

"Well I think I blew it…I got ticked off and wanted him to know I was close enough to slap him into oblivion. He freaked out and went inside. Your telephone is on the front porch…I have business…see you later."

I was surprised I didn't blow up at her and more surprised that I even talked to her. I was glad I didn't let on that I knew anything about what she's been doing to me. When I first saw the Subaru coming my way, I was going to just ignore her and drive right on by, but at the last second I stopped, I don't know, must come with age.

Maybe some of all those little sayings you hear are starting to mean more to me. Especially that one about picking up a rattle snake and being surprised that it bites you. The point is that you knew what it was when you picked it up, it was a rattle snake, and that is what rattle snakes do.

Originally, I was kind to Britney because I wanted to change her. But whether it's done forcefully, or with kindness and tolerance, trying to change someone is still manipulation and control. I tried to change Britney because I thought change was what she wanted, but she didn't want to change. She only wanted what changing would bring her. I went off by myself to sulk and try to think what to do with this snake in my back yard. I was the one who let her in. I couldn't be upset with her for being there.

I was driving my Saab, Britney had my Subaru. There was no need to go anywhere together. We still had our Extended Stay on the north side, but I hadn't been there for three days.

Since my talk with Damon I went to all the clubs that San Ji might be found. I didn't ask for him or mention his name. I didn't want everyone in town to know I was looking for him. I wasn't sure what I was going to do when I saw him.

I didn't see myself doing what I said I would do but I took the payment for it. I saw an article about suicide once. It said that most suicides were really accidents. It said that those people who attempted suicide were doing just that, *attempting* suicide. They didn't really want to succeed with actually doing it. They wanted someone to see the attempt and care enough about them to stop them. But sooner or later, they would come too close, and go too far. And sooner or later there would be no one to talk them out of it, or to save the day.

I thought about how those things we plan, or start to do on purpose, actually being accomplished by accident. I don't actually want to kill anyone, and certainly not San Ji. But still, I've gone such a dangerous distance, holding on to a critical decision that would need to be made in a split second.

I wondered; are some homicides accidents too?

I tried to hate…I tried to get mad…I tried logic.

I even tried religion and prayed, "Dear Lord, if I am not supposed to do this make the bullet miss, make the gun jam, or stop me in some way." I felt free to go forward with me self discovery, knowing God would not let me make the wrong decision. Could it be I was an instrument of punishment San Ji was supposed to face?

I told myself that at least it's me, and not someone else, working for Michaels. The apprehension I had about the whole deal was in San Ji's favor. I doubt that anyone else would have given this as much thought as I had. And then, if it happens, it was supposed to happen. I wondered what it felt like…killing someone.

I heard where he might be found.

I went back by my room. I saw that Britney hadn't been back in the past four days either, so I called her, "Come on by, I want to talk to you about something."

That same evening she showed.

We never asked each other where we were, it just wasn't like that. I told her that whether or not I got out of this trouble, I was going to move to

Ellijay and if she wanted to go with me we would have to start going to church, and we would have to start living a quiet life in the country.

I asked her, "What do you think about that?"

She seemed genuinely happy, "Oh yes…can we get a cabin or something…you know, live in the hills?" Then she laughed and said, "We'll be *hillbillies.*" Everything was a game to her and she always liked what we did at first, but then it was always the same old, *are we there yet* boredom when the first five minutes were up.

"If that's what you want…yes we'll be *hillbillies.* If that's what we have to do to put this life behind us. OK? I've had my fill of it and I know it for what it is. It's a trap. You ask for something and life gives it to you, now how cruel can that be?"

Britney skewed her face and cocked her head much like a puzzled Cocker Spaniel but with more expression.

I raised my voice and shouted softly, "I feel like yelling, *God don't do me any favors.* Don't give me what I want, you know what I need. I'm not strong enough to go for what I need on my own. It might mean hard work, discipline and sacrifice. Quit giving me what I want and give me what I need."

By the expression on her face I could see that Britney still didn't understand a word I said. I don't think I did either. Because, right then, I was just making noise. It was right then, at that moment, that I was making a major decision. I had already gone the distance with her by marrying her, and all this noise was just to drown out the voice that was telling me not to go that extra mile, not for her.

But, my life had already gone so far down the tubes that any 'extra' mile to go, was way behind me, now. I was committed in a direction so badly bent for hell,

When Britney chimed in, I saw a Shirley Temple as a child, imitating a cause for which she was too young to understand. With chin dug into her chest, lips pushed out, and a playful scowl across her brow, she said, in the deepest tone her voice could go, "That's right…don't do *us* no favors".

But it wasn't any child star at all saying that, it was the innocence of a fourteen year old little girl before the eleven years of prostitution turned her into a snake. When that innocence smiled at me I couldn't find the anger in me, for any of the treacherous, conniving, despicable things she had done.

I, simply, could not hate her.

After all, she might be just a snake...but, in all the world...she was all I had.

22

We slept until midnight and then packed all our things in the Subaru. We drove both cars to Hapeville so we could put a 'For Sale' sign on the Saab and park it at Joe's club he so creatively named Joe's Place. This served two purposes. This gave me a place to leave my car and I heard San Ji might be there.

Britney and I walked into Joe's through the back door and the minute Joe saw us he started yelling, "Get out of here man. Quick…run. They were just here."

"Whoa. Who was here?"

"Fulton County."

"I thought Cobb County was looking for me."

"They heard you been here…"

I said, "Wait a minute man…but why all this? They taking a warrant on me everywhere I go?"

"You broke that cops thumb when you jumped out that window in Cobb…'

"Ooooh, you gotta be joking. They upset about that?"

Joe pointed to Britney and said, "They said you're forcing Britney to go with you…kidnapping or something. They know you have that Mossberg, a .44 Bulldog, and a 9mm. They're going to dust you on sight."

"That's ridiculous…tell him baby…I'm not forcing you…"

"Don't tell me. I mean it, man, they were here just a minute ago" Joe went to the back door and looked out and then turned and waved me over, "Ok go. Go on, get out a here."

I was starting to get that scary chilled feeling in my chest and gut again. That feeling that takes your breath away at the anticipation that something almost has you. I saw that hand grabbing me just before I hit the briars that night in December. "What the hell," I yelled, "they're coming after me like I'm mass a murderer, or something."

"One more thing Duke…when they come up on you, put your hands up and lay down. They flatly said they're going to blow you away. They know you're armed and they said they already know you're going to try to take them down so don't resist, and don't run, just put your hands up and lay down. I know these guys, they'll do it and then brag about how they were the one to take down the Duke…they're punks."

"Say, can I leave my Saab on your…"

"Leave it…now go…just go. I'll pull it around back. Call me in a day or two."

As we pulled onto the freeway I told Britney, "One more stop…"

"Then we go to Ellijay?"

"That's right baby then we go north and find God."

I drove to Back Streets to check for San Ji. We pulled into a far corner of the lot and sat in the car for a minute after parking. I looked at Britney and for the first time I believe I saw her feeling some relief about getting away from Atlanta. I'm sure she hadn't the faintest idea of what I was thinking as I stared at her. As I took my time watching the back of my fingers glide down across her cheek I wondered what was wrong with me. My hand went around the back of her neck and I pulled her head towards my chest and laid my head back on the head rest and closed my eyes and thought…this is the one who has been trying to bury me.

It was probably my imagination but I thought I began to see her changing to my side. I saw in her what appeared to be a desire to get on some right track of life, whatever that would be. I didn't know what that "right track" would be, but Britney didn't know that I didn't know, and so she appeared to be content to follow me, whatever track I took us on. And if for no other reason, but to have someone who would follow the likes of me, I bought into my imagination.

I saw my chance to hate her slipping further and further away.

Before we got out of the car I held her hand and said a prayer. It wasn't a very long prayer, or a fancy one, but it was a prayer. I remember thinking that this was our first prayer and so it must mean something special.

In this prayer I merely asked God to have Damon drop the charges so I could beat this phony armed robbery rap. I asked God to help me find San

Ji, so I could handle the job I needed to do, in the way God thought it should go.

Britney raised her head, opened one eye and said, "What's that about San Ji?"

"Nothing baby…now hush."

She closed her eyes and lowered her head.

I continued, "God help us get to Ellijay and thank you for Ben Kiker. Amen."

Britney said, "Wait a minute," and quickly added, "Watch over my mother and father and help my sister get away from that dope head Scott. Now, amen."

"Very good, now let's go inside."

This prayer must have inspired Britney because she wanted to tell me that she was reading a book I gave her a few weeks ago.

"That book I'm reading is really a good book" she said, "I like it."

"What book?"

"That book you said I could borrow…remember? We were going through some of your things in storage."

"I don't remember any…"

"Oh, you knooow…that book…it was *Words about Living*…or loving or something like that."

"Oh yeah, that was *the Living Word*…that was the bible, baby, the New Testament."

"Well I like it. It sure is a good book."

I smiled at this kid who I keep forgetting is my wife and I shook my head.

We got out and walked by a car where a couple was shooting up in the back seat. The guy saw me looking and he smiled a sheepish grin, I nodded and smiled back. Britney made some off-color remark, about Scott doping up her sister, as she passed them.

We went into the club that was filled with pimps, whores, and drug dealers. But we went in all prayed up. And I guess I didn't really have much room to criticize any one else; after all, I was there to kill someone.

23

San Ji was supposed to be at Back Streets. I didn't really know what I would do when I saw him. I thought to leave that entirely up to God. I knew if I was not supposed to kill him, God would stop me from doing it. I don't know how, but somehow He would stop me. And I didn't want Britney to be there if I went through with it.

"Britney, let's do some Krispy Kreme, what do you say?"

"Krispy Kreme? Gee…that's all the way downtown."

"We *are* downtown Brit."

"Oh, we are, aren't we, Ok, what do you want?"

"You know what I like, just take your time. Let me take care of business."

She frowned and cocked her head to one side and I saw the question coming, "What business? We are going aren't we?"

"Yes baby, we're going. Just run on to Krispy Kreme."

I didn't inquire as to San Ji's whereabouts but I did a pretty thorough search of the place. I checked up stairs, in the lounge and around the three dance floors and in all the dark corners that hold people you never knew were there.

San Ji wasn't there.

I resigned myself to kill some time playing pool while waiting for Britney to get back. When she returned I had just finished playing three games of pool with Bobby. We hardly spoke the whole time, Bobby and I.

"I know who you are," was a strange thing for this black dude to say to me. He stood extremely close to me as he chalked his cue stick, and leaning in a little closer he whispered again, over my left shoulder, "I said…I know who you are."

I stepped away from him towards the table and lined up my next shot. Without looking at him I asked, "So Bobby, who am I?"

Bobby and I met a couple months before and it wasn't a good meeting. We were at the Palace and I was so wasted on ecstasy I could hardly stand up. I didn't know Bobby at that time but he approached me and feigned a friendly handshake.

"Hi, my name is Bobby, Bobby Truett." He held onto my hand and began pulling my arm rapidly in different directions as he pumped my arm up and down in a mock handshake trying to make me fall over. He was too stupid to know that I was only able to stand up because he had a hold of my hand. All he had to do was to let go of my hand and I would have fallen on my face and looked even more the fool.

At the time, I couldn't tell if he was trying to provoke me or if he was being friendly and was just playing with me. I didn't take my eyes off him as my surprised look turned into a smile, "Do I know you?"

The bouncer walked up and said something to him and he let go of my hand and disappeared into the crowd. The bouncer winked at me and apologized. I dismissed the whole thing as something not important enough to try to understand.

Bobby came into the Palace a week later. He approached me with a smile and wanted to shake hands. I looked at him coldly, without accepting his hand, and all I said to him was, "You have one minute to get out of here."

He turned around and walked out, and that was that.

Now there we were again, crossing paths, this time at "Back Streets". I saw him earlier but I let it pass as he did with me. "Back Streets" is not a good place to start any trouble. The club caters to the gay and lesbian crowd and the management is particularly sensitive to trouble of a violent nature. The slightest disturbance and you're off to jail. That's why Back Streets is a good mellowing out watering hole. You go there when you want to catch your breath, or when you want to exhale, and chill out for awhile.

We found ourselves facing each other on the pool table. I ignored him and didn't give any sign of recollecting our brief history. I put the quarters in and he racked the balls and we acted as though we never saw each other before now. Just as I was getting ready to break, Bobby took a cautious step in my direction and when he was within striking distance he totally surprised me.

He spoke! "Hey man, I want to apologize for the way I acted at the Palace."

He completely threw me off guard.

I may have been angry with Bobby, but he was no slacker. He had a following and quite a reputation and here he just apologized to me. You don't see that around here.

I was impressed, and if the truth were to be known, I was relieved.

I accepted his apology.

He put four stacks of quarters on the rail of the pool table reserving his place for the next four games, "I have a proposition for you."

We played two games without speaking to each other and were now on the third game. I made the 6-ball in the corner pocket and was lining up my next shot. The game was going to be over soon and I hadn't heard anything like a proposition yet.

Bobby came up close to me again and said, "I know who you are."

Instead of taking my shot I stood up and grabbed the chalk and said, "Oh? Really?"

"Look man," and he began, "I'm a good man to have around. When I make a pick-up, all the cash gets to where it's supposed to be. If the guy needs a lesson, he gets it. If he needs to disappear, I can take care of that too. My work is clean…no worry to it. I dig my holes so deep no one finds a thing. That means nothing is coming back on anyone. Like I say…I'm good."

He stopped talking and looked me in the eye and waited.

When I didn't say anything he said, "So?"

"So? So what?

"Hey man, I apologized to you. There's no need holding a grudge."

"That's not the problem here, Bobby. So you say you're good…how do I know you're good?"

"Give me a chance…I'll show you how good."

"Who knows you?" I shrugged. "I don't know you. I just know you did a stupid thing. It's not that I'm pissed about it. It was just stupid. If you were working with me and did something like that we'd both fry."

"I made a mistake."

I chalked up my cue and didn't answer. I was thinking about this Bobby Truett guy. How bad could a person be when they admit they made a mistake? I was thinking about what was happening right then. I couldn't help but think how cool it was. Here's a guy who discovered something about me since the last time we met, and now he wants to work with me.

He saw in the way I was pondering this thought that he was close to closing the deal and so he hurriedly added, "Look man, I didn't know who you were, that was stupid of me. I know who you are now. We could work things good together, man."

I don't know if I was starting to like this guy, or if I was getting big headed about how badly he wanted to work with me, and then maybe, it was a little bit of both.

But then there was north Georgia and my plan to lead Britney to Christ. It seemed I was moving into a different status level here, with Bobby Truett applying for a job with me. Evidently my image on the street has taken a turn for the better, and wouldn't it be a lot better if we had a bit more cash once we got to Ellijay? I really wouldn't need to hide out that bad just yet, not if I put San Ji off for awhile.

"I tell you what, Bobby. How 'bout I call you sometime when I got something that needs doing. You ride with me one night; we can see how "good" you are."

Bobby's cool fell apart as he hurried to get a pen from the bar. He looked like a teenage kid who just got his first job sweeping floors at Burger King. His excitement flattered me and I got the number to his cell phone and left my cue stick on the table. We didn't finish the game.

Our business was finished and so was our beer and so I grabbed Britney and we left. I was anxious to get away and absorb what just went down.

I was surprised for feeling so proud of this new level to which I had just fallen. Someone who says he has experience along the same lines as I, fervently applied for a position with me. I was afraid if I turned him down I'd lose the powerful rush it gave my ego.

I wanted to say to Britney, "See...see what people think of me." But instead I just said "Want to get a drink?"

Britney asked, "Where are we going?"

"Crazy Horse."

"We're not going to north Georgia?"

"Nope...Crazy Horse."

Britney was silent as she thought about it. "Hey, do you think they'll give me a job?" She grabbed her T-shirt and pulled it up above her neck and laughed, "Look, I'd be a good dancer...huh?"

"You'd be a great dancer baby...I'll talk to Mike...we'll see."

24

There was a kind of "tiredness" about me that I rarely felt. It was as though my desire was constantly coming up short, and my energy level was being drained because of it.

I was tired of my life standing still, I was tired of it running a mile a minute, and I was just tired of my life.

Where was that powerful feeling I was afraid of losing thirty minutes ago? My ego was being stroked by Bobby Truett showing me he was less than me, and now; I felt exhausted because of it.

There's something very tiring in the pursuit of such an empty life.

"What's wrong with you...huh?" Britney had a puzzled look on her face.

I parked the car in the rear of the Crazy Horse and sat there lost to the thought of what life might be like in Ellijay. "I don't know baby, I'm just tired all of a sudden. You go on in...check with Mama. You know Mama?"

"You mean the lady that looks after the girls?"

"Yeah, ask her if they're looking for any girls and then when I come in I'll ask Mike for you. I'll be there in a minute."

When Britney went inside, the parking lot took on a stillness that I envied. The power of it was scary and made me want to look behind me, and when I did, it only left me wanting to look again.

A cop car turned its lights and siren on and raced past the club down Jonesboro road and onto the freeway. The siren faded into the stillness and there I sat, just a little old man...lost inside this little black car, in the darkness behind a low class bar with pretty lights out front.

Somehow, I was able to see myself sitting there and I wondered how could I tell anyone who I really was? How could I tell anyone that I really don't want this life without blowing them away? If I told anyone I wasn't who they thought I was, no one would want to "ride" with me. No one would think I was "the man" I want them to think I am.

How utterly small I felt and what a tremendous impact the thought of being so insignificant had on my life at that moment.

The moments in my life would just be decisions to do this, or do that, go here or go there. And even though the proper thing to do was already known, it was actually doing what had to be done that would give what was "known" any value at all. *Knowing* is one thing, but it is what is done about what is known that makes all the difference in the world.

I'd been carrying my bible around because I knew it held something good for me but I hadn't spent much time in it. I had many things to pray about and I knew prayer could help me, but I didn't pray as I should have. The only thing I thought I *knew* and was *doing* that was right, was leading a girl to live a Christian life, but I hadn't really done that yet either.

I told my friend in Ellijay, "Ben, I'm leading this young girl to the Lord. And as soon as I get on my feet I'm going to get my Spiritual Survival video going and I'm going to get active with my Christian Karate Academy. I'm going to be on fire for the Lord."

Ben said, "Duke, that's all well and good, but to tell you the truth, all that isn't necessary. God just wants you."

"No Ben, you watch, you'll see. I got Britney off the street and I'll..."

Ben interrupted, "Duke, all that God needs is *you*. Can't you see that?"

"But what about..."

"Duke, listen to me, if God had you...if God really had your heart, people would see it in the way you lived your life. Once they saw God in you, then God would have them too. But it has to start with you."

I wasn't sure I understood what Ben was telling me. That seemed to me to be a bit selfish to just think about myself and think that God just wanted me. For some reason or another that conversation had been repeated in my thinking over and over in the past few days.

If I went to Ellijay I could work and get an attorney and get all this stuff cleared up without tripping over anything new. But then I'd need money to start with and I already got paid for this job I'm to do and I guess I just need to stick around and do it.

Knowing what to do was fading fast, and the "doing" of anything that would help, was lost a long time ago…

I got out of the car and went inside. The bouncer on the door called Mike's office and then told me to go on back. As I was taking a seat on the couch to the right of his desk, Mike said, "I guess you heard about San Ji."

"Nah, what's he done this time?" Before he answered I remembered my promise to Britney, "Oh yeah, before I forget, I told Britney I would ask you if you could use anyone. She wants to be a dancer.'

"We always have room for another dancer. They're either always leaving or just forgetting where they work. Not the most responsible bunch. You don't mind her dancing here…doing lap dances? Because that's where the money is."

"She has always done what ever she's wanted. I'm not going to change her, and now she wants to dance. I pretty much give up.

Mike knew where Britney came from and said, "She can't be hustling on her own around here. We don't allow the girls to leave with the customers."

"Listen Mike, I'm going to tell you…if you could use her, fine. If not, that's Ok too. If you hire her it's not doing me a thing one way or the other. I told her I'd ask you, but know up front she's going to be a problem. If you have to fire her…fire her, no hard feelings."

"I'll be straight with you Duke; a lot of the girls set up their dates and meet them somewhere away from the club. If that's her habit, which I've heard it was, she'll be right back in it, working here. If you can live with…"

I raised hand and stopped Mike from finishing. I shook my head, "Nah, you're right, won't work, hold up on the job. But don't tell her I said so. I'll just say there wasn't an opening and I got you to put her on a waiting list or something. It wouldn't be a good idea for her to be working here…so what's San Ji done now?"

"He's dead."

I jumped up off the couch, "What?"

"I thought you knew…"

"Knew? How would I know? I haven't seen him man…really. I have not seen him…I bet it's been weeks…really you got to believe that…I haven't…"

"Wait…wait…wait a minute, man…chill out."

I sat back down and took a deep breath and let it out, "So he's dead…Huh?"

"Yep…cops got him."

"Cops?" I started to jump up again and caught myself, "What cops?"

"The Red Dog Squad man. They got him, down at Jackson Lake."

"What? Why, what happened?"

Mike asked, "Well…you *know* about San don't you?"

I wasn't sure but all the signs pointed to it and so I guessed, "You mean…?" and I made a circle in the air, over and over, with my hand.

"Yeah, he was rolling. That's why he always had those new faces around him and that's why he could operate so much in the open."

Early on, I had the idea that the bad times San Ji told me about had to do with him getting arrested. That was in the day that I gave him a strip of rawhide on which hung the memorabilia that I thought protected me. He said it protected him.

He must have made a deal to lighten his sentence and "rollover" on the people with whom he did business. He was allowed to function as usual with the DEA's "product" and although he had to account for the money there was always plenty of money to put away for when he got out.

"You know…" I unconsciously lifted my hand to feel a yin yang medallion, a crystal, and a painted feather against my chest, "we were talking on the phone one time. I was mad at him for giving Kiwi a new van for Christmas, that's before I was out of the picture, anyway he said, *'so what, I gave five other girls a new car too'*. I didn't know what to say; it sure didn't console me that he gave five other girls cars. I don't care how many other girls he gave a car, I was mad that he gave my girl a car. A few beats went by and not knowing anything else to say I said, *'San Ji, you know you're going to get caught don't you?'* and I could hear the cockiness in his tone as he said in that soft voice that mixed his Korean accent with a southern drawl, '*Well Duke…we're aaaall going to get caught. It's just a matter of how you prepare for it.*"

Mike smiled and nodded his head as he listened, "Yeah that fits with what I heard. I wondered how he could operate so much in the open."

I said, "The cops wanted him to operate as much in the open as he could. It brought the people he dealt with out in he open. I remember one time, in the parking lot, right in front of the front door of the Palace, Mark slipped him a big rock…on the sly. You know? San Ji opened his hand in front of everyone standing there and said real loud, 'What's this? This ain't nothing, you trying to insult me?' But it was a good rock. A good size rock, at least an eight ball of solid red geek rock. San Ji made a big deal of how puny it was and then reared back and threw it as far as he could. He threw it into the woods next to the club."

Mike laughed, "Was Tank there? He probably went screaming into the woods after it."

I continued, "Then he took us into his van and opened up a lock box with a dozen huge rocks. It had to be at least two or three pounds of speed, rocks the size of baseballs."

Mike said, "Well, he spent all his money on women and gambling and…"

I interrupted, "I'm telling ya…the past few times I saw him at the Palace he looked bad, man. Real bad." I suddenly felt exposed and I sensed my excitement gave off an awkward energy because I imagined everyone would know what Michaels paid me to do.

I couldn't slow myself down though, "He wore an old smelly T-shirt and dirty jeans…must have been up for a week or more…his eyes were dark and sunk back into his skull…bad man…*real* bad." I talked too fast and wondered if it was noticeable.

But when Mike chimed in at his quick pace, I wondered what it was he had to hide. Mike lifted an eyebrow and cocked his head towards me, "Doing too much of his own 'product' if you ask me, and spending too much on the strippers and the gambling.

I added, "So what could you expect?"

Mike continued his story, "When the cops pulled his chain and said it was time to go, he didn't have anything put away for when he got out. So he ran. They chased him to Jackson Lake. The report is that he swam out and drowned himself; but Duke…c'mon man, he ran his car into a tree on the edge of the lake…both of his legs were broken, man…c'mon. If you could even get out of your car how are you going to get to the water? And then how far are you going to swim with two broke legs?"

"So what are you saying?"

There went the eyebrow again. Mike looked at me like I was a moron for asking, "C'mon Duke someone dragged him out of the car and threw him in the lake. He couldn't swim nowhere in his condition."

This first thing that came up came out, "Who?"

Mike shot me that glance again and said something as he turned away.

I didn't hear Mike's response. I was hearing Joe telling me to drop to the ground if the cops catch me because they were going to kill me for the sport of it. When Joe told me that, I didn't believe it for a minute. I thought, *"What? Cops would do that?"* I thought back on the cops who were stealing the safes and dumping them in Jackson Lake and wondered how, if, or why San Ji was rolling on those guys.

I turned my attention back to Mike just in time to hear him say, "We all die to some degree in some way every day and there's a part of my life I'm laying aside for San Ji; that part of me has been fully paid…with memories of times well spent".

It was a good thing I couldn't see the expression on my face when I heard Mike say that. I can only imagine the shocked look I must have had. This was a dead serious time but I thought Mike must have been cracking a joke or being sarcastic.

He wasn't.

"Times well spent?" Where did that come from? I felt like I was a senior in college, talking to some kid in Kindergarten, and I was hearing something I would have said a hundred years ago. But, *"Well spent"? This*, was time well spent?

All of a sudden I felt my age. I shook my head and let out a breath, "Whew, you know Mike…I think I'm going to go get Britney…we need to get on out of here. I got Clayton, Cobb, Fulton and now Dekalb breathing down my neck. I don't want to end up in Jackson Lake…gotta go…catch you later."

"Maybe not man, in a couple days I'm out of here."

"Oh?" Here was someone else wanting out. I was interested. "Where you going?"

"Montana…got family up there…lives out near Bozeman…just flat land man. Quiet, peaceful, clean air and no drama. Nothing at all like here, you know, it's healthy living. You know what I mean…the good life that I use to think was boring. No more of this crap. I might just pick up and go man. Yeah, maybe I'll just go…" he stopped talking for a minute but his head kept bobbing up and down as if my response was going to help him confirm a decision being made inside him right then.

As I watched that decision being made, I stood and looked at Mike and for the first time I saw a human being. I didn't say anything. I just slowly nodded my head up and down in unison with his and smiled. I slowly stepped back into the office and shook Mike's hand. I held it tightly for a second and smiled with envy, "God bless you Mike. I hope you go through with it…really. Get on outta here and when you go, don't go back into the club business."

I felt a sadness coming up and so I turned and walked away quickly. I grit my teeth and looked disgusted at the nine to fivers gawking at the naked teenage girls. By the time I reached the outside door I felt a strong anger mix with this sadness that was building up in me.

I knew the sadness that was rising in me, wasn't because Mike was going away. I didn't know Mike well enough to miss him. The sadness was that someone I knew had the guts to get out of this life, and I was still going to be here.

25

Britney asked, "So what are you all mad about?"

"I'm not mad."

"Did you see those fat hogs dancing? I'd be a good dancer. What'd Mike say?"

There wasn't anyway Britney would understand my reasoning for anything I was doing so I made up a reason for looking mad, "Oh that damn Mike...said he didn't need any dancers.

"Britney jumped to the edge of her seat and turned towards me, "Oh yes they do, Mama said so. He's a liar."

"I know. I know. I think it's cuz I'm on the run and he doesn't want me around here."

"You don't have to come around."

"He's not going to do it, Britney...we're *both* too hot. The last thing a club wants is a reason for cops to come around. If you work here they'd just watch the club and that's bad for business."

She plopped back into the seat and crossed her arms, "So what are we going to do now?" She quickly fell into a deep pout and with as much sarcasm as she could make work for her she said, "Sooo...big shot...are we still...*getting out of dodge?*"

I grit my teeth and stomped on the accelerator and glared at the road ahead.

"It's your problem, ya know...it's you they're after. Why do I have to go? I could make some good money dancing, I know I could."

I tried to understand why I thought I had someone worth helping in this selfish pathetic soul who, all this time, has been trying her best to bury me.

Her mood changed abruptly, "I'm hungry. Let's stop and get something to eat. We going to Ellijay now?"

"I *want* to; I know it's what we should do." I wasn't sure what I was feeling and I couldn't explain it very well so I just said, "Not knowing what Damon's going to do, and then there's you. I just don't know about you; and well, I just don't know about anything right now."

"What do you mean? What *about* me?"

I didn't answer.

Her eyes widen and she slowly turned her head away while keeping her eyes fixed on me. What she must have sensed was what right and so she inched across the seat towards the door and quit talking.

My mind was racing with thoughts of San Ji and Michaels and this stupid gun inside the glove. I can go give the money back and be broke but I thought of how badly we needed money. I remembered the nights we spent our last penny on a dozen Krispy Kreme donuts and ate the whole box before leaving the parking lot. They really fill you up and the sugar takes the craving away. I didn't want to go back to being that broke again, but I didn't want to hurt anyone any more, either.

There was a funny sort of selfish anger that confused me. I never thought I would have pulled the trigger on San Ji but I wanted to prove it to myself. I wanted to find him and face this person, who I've become, by facing what I might do. A tear pushed out from where they gathered and went over the edge. I quickly wiped my eye and blinked the rest away. I felt the strangest form of guilt for wanting to use San Ji to prove to myself that I hadn't fallen that far.

I visualized the way I thought it might have turned out; maybe we would laugh it off, and I would prove to be even a greater friend to him for warning him, and then we would devise Michael's demise. But now, I won't ever really know...I selfishly mourned the loss of the opportunity to try and recapture something still good in me. I selfishly mourned that loss of me, more than I mourned the loss of my friend.

Because of the way things went down, I felt too closely connected to his death

Who will Michaels send after me if I stiff him for the money? He's going to know it wasn't me that killed San Ji. Maybe I should keep the money and go against Michaels before he sends someone after me.

Mike said Ji's death was already in the papers, and as I think of it now, I doubt that I was the only one Michaels sent after San Ji.

San Ji was the one who *accidentally* rolled over on the cops that were hitting the clubs and stealing their safes and here he ends up in Jackson Lake where the safes were found. San Ji didn't drown himself, that's ridiculous. How much strength would it take to go down and purposely drown your self? I believe Mike was right, the cops did it. The only witnesses to him swimming out to the middle and drowning himself were cops.

How much allegiance do I owe Michaels anyway? I doubt very much that this gun in the brown glove is clean. I wonder whose finger prints are on the gun in the glove. What was the purpose of me killing San Ji, *with this gun*? Who else was going to fry because of me?

"Where we going?" Britney held on to her guarded expression. I sensed she knew that I knew about her and I saw that she was scared.

I didn't answer her but I did reach over and hold her hand and smile.

That appeared to scare her more so I said, "I don't know sweetheart, I don't know, jut let me think."

She moved back towards me and wrapped her arms around my arm and laid her head on my shoulder.

Rocky was going to set Hot Rod up for me and I would have to break his hands if he didn't have the money. I'll just break one I thought, I'll get it over quick. But if he has the money I'll get $1000 of it and I'll have enough to give Michaels back most of his money.

After that I'll get out and stay out.

Again my head wasn't thinking right.

The night I jumped out the window and ran from four cops I first thought to jump back in bed, and pretend to be asleep. Then I thought I should get dressed. Finally, while my life was seconds away from being finished, I tried to remove the screen from the window without damaging it.

These thoughts came back to me because I was doing the same thing now. I was panicking then, and I'm doing it again. I'm planning to do things that make no sense at all.

I was unsure of what to do, but I kept putting 'one foot in front of the other' and headed towards Rocky's house in the country. There wasn't the usual milling around of dark and shady figures. The house was empty and every room in the house was dark, but I couldn't shake the feeling that there were people I couldn't see, lurking in the shadows.

Rocky took us downstairs and into what looked to be his bedroom. He said, "Stay here, I'll set things up. I'll be back in the morning."

He didn't get back until late the next afternoon but he said he had good news. "I got to talking with Hot Rod and he told me what he was into and said he was just getting ready to pay some guy he owes. How much does he owe your guy?"

"Two grand."

"That's him. He said he would bring it by tonight."

"When?"

"Later on, but you can't be here. You'll spook him. He's on to you. He knows you're looking for him. How about you take Billy's car and split. Call me after nine O'clock tonight, I'll get the money and you come on by then and I'll give it to you. Don't drive your car; cops are looking for that black Subaru. Take Billy's. Pick your car up when you head out to wherever you're going."

"Man, I really appreciate this Rocky."

"Go on, now. Give me a call after nine."

I left all my things and Britney's black garbage bag in the trunk of the Subaru and took my Mossberg shotgun and the brown glove with the gun in it. There was something strange going on and I really didn't care what it was. I felt free for some reason and I didn't know why. I had the $1500 from Michaels hidden in the spare tire in the trunk of my Subaru because I didn't want to touch it until I knew what I was going to do with it, but I had a ten dollar bill in my pocket.

"Britney, could you go for a dozen Krispy Kreme's?"

She never knew about the hidden money and so she jumped on the donut run. We filled ourselves with Krispy Kremes and drove around aimlessly waiting for the time to call Rocky.

As we came up to a shopping center, I saw a familiar sign in the far corner of the mall. I pulled in and parked a fair distance from Joe Corley's Karate Studio and told Britney to wait in the car.

When I entered the front door, everyone in the parents waiting area turned to look at me. On the other side of the thick glass partition there was a karate class going on. I walked over to the corner of the glass partition that led out onto the mat. I stood there and watched class.

An office door opened to my left and I saw Joe Corley come out of his office. As he walked towards me, I looked him straight in the face and was ready to say hello, but; although he looked straight at me, he walked past me without saying a word. He passed again and this time he nearly bumped into me, but he still didn't say anything.

Joe knows me. I helped train Joe for his World Championship fight with Bill Wallace. When I had trouble in my marriage I slept on Joe's couch.

Joe knows me.

He came out of his office again and this time I looked across the work out area and into the five foot tall mirror that ran the length of the room and I watched him. When he was passing me I saw him pass a man in the mirror that had on a long leather coat.

This man wore a leather jacket under a long leather coat and he wore black combat fatigues that were tied at the ankles. He had work-out gloves with the fingers cut out and one hand held on to some long object under his coat. He wore a red bandanna and a ball cap turned backwards. I thought I recognized except for the wild eyed expression of surprise on his face.

He was there, in the mirror.

Joe was passing him, at the same time, Joe was passing me.

"Oh, I know who you are" I whispered to myself.

I shook my head and let out a breath I didn't know I was holding. I walked over to a counter where a lead box was sitting. I found a pen on the counter and wrote, "Joe if you were ever in the business of saving souls…I need help." I signed my name and put the note in the lead box on the counter.

I left, to go break someone's hands, or collect his due.

There was an aura of depression around me. I didn't really care what happened anymore. I wasn't sure if I was disappointed in the type of person I saw myself to be, or if I was just upset that someone else killed San Ji, and now I'll never know how much I have really fallen.

As I crossed the lot to my car I was getting mad again.

"I could have done it," I muttered to myself. "But I wouldn't have. I could...but I wouldn't...I know I wouldn't."

Britney said, "What'd you say?"

"Just talking to myself baby...just to myself..." I got in and slammed the door.

"Someone say something to you? What's wrong?"

"Nothing Britney...nothing..." I was yelling at her and I squealed the tires as we pulled out onto the surface street.

"Look who's speeding now," she said.

I pulled back into the lot and got out and went around the car, "You drive...and don't speed. I'll call Rocky."

Rocky told me to pull into the truck stop on I-285 when I got back to the other side of town and he would bring me the money.

"What about my car?"

"I'll drive your car there and we'll swap cars at the truck stop and it will be a done deal. You'll have your money, your car and you can go on your way."

I said, "That's sweet. I'm on my way."

26

What happens in each moment we live will dictate what happens in the next moment to come. Good, bad, small or large, we can't live in this moment without going through the one that went before it.

So, whether we recognize it or not, we're literally living from moment to moment.

There is a lifetime in that moment we just lived; a whole life in that split second that just raced past us…It was not just another idle moment in time…it was our life. We better catch it or find a way to settle back and let it catch us, and if we can, we better live that moment (that life) as though it meant something.

Live it now, before it too, races out of sight.

We parked in a space around to the side of the truck stop and waited for Rocky. I let my front seat back and put my hands behind my head and put one foot up on the dash. I sat back and got comfortable and said, "Britney, Jesus said to his disciples when he was telling them of His fate of having to die on the cross, *You see me now but soon you will see me no more.*"

"Huh?"

"Wow, do you see what He was saying? He was Life."

"Life?"

"Britney, have you ever felt lost?"

Losing her curiosity in the questions Britney shrugged, "Oh, I don't know. A lot of times I guess…are you hungry?"

"I mean…your whole life, you know, as though you're just not getting anywhere."

"Don't know, haven't lived my whole life yet." She looked over at me, "What are you saying? You feeling old or something?"

"No…I don't mean just that…"

She laughed as a new thought just came to her, "Wow…do you realize that by the time I'm your age…you're going to be dead?" She got a big laugh out of that one and then added, "Oooh…weee baby…how about that, huh?"

Honesty used to hurt me until I met Britney. I learned to take an honest look at a lot of things about myself that would have scared me before. But she always told me how it was, straight out, no sugar coating. I once said I really liked that honesty, but to tell you the truth, I sure wish the details of what was true about me was different at times.

"I was just thinking about this idea of being lost. Have you ever heard the story about the prodigal son?"

"The what?"

"The prodigal son. It's a story from the bible."

"I guess not…you hungry?"

"There's a Wendy's in the truck stop. But listen; the story of the prodigal son is known as the parable of the lost son."

"You're losing me now. I don't know them words, what's a parable?"

"Britney, just listen, you can get the idea of what it means by listening. You don't need to know the definition of every word."

Talking to her frustrated me.

She said, "I'm just trying to learn and how do you know Rocky isn't setting you up?"

"C'mon, why would he do a thing like that?"

"You hardly know him."

"I hardly know anybody. I don't even know you, Britney, and I married you. Now, are you going to settle down when we get to Ellijay?"

"All depends what you mean by *settle down*."

"You know, let's stay away from the clubs, the drugs, alcohol. We'll just live, you and me."

"And God! Don't forget God."

"Well, of course, God, that's what I mean."

We had enough money for a large order of Fries at Wendy's and we sat back in the car and split it as we waited for Rocky.

"I know about the Prodigal Son," Britney said as she stuffed a hand full of fries in her mouth. "He left home and his folks were glad to see him when he came back. I remember that story. I think I'm prodigal sometimes," she paused, "but I can't go home."

"Why's that?"

"My mother hates me. I visit once in a while but she hates me."

"Oh no, now, Britney, I can't believe that. Why would your own mother hate you?"

"When I was young my dad would get drunk and sneak into my room and do me. He started doing that when I was 10 years old. He did that for a year and I finally couldn't take it anymore and I told my mother. She called me a liar and threw me out of the house. Now, my dad's mad at me and my mother hates me."

Britney wasn't mad, she wasn't sad, she just told me. Dry eyed and without emotion; she just told me. She crammed another handful of fries in her mouth.

I waited a long moment before saying anything, "Well, the Prodigal son wasn't only about his folks being glad to see him come home. And it wasn't that he was poor or had to live in poverty. He had a good home when he left. His father was rich but he ended up a lot like us. We're not exactly eating with the pigs, we got our Krispy Kreme and all, but I see a lot of "us" in that story, but I also see a way out that really makes sense." I paused and thought carefully what I just said.

Britney seemed interested, "What do you see?"

"Well, Britney, look at us. Just look at what we're doing, we're going down the wrong road."

"But aren't we going to Ellijay?"

"Yeah, but only because I can see what happened with the prodigal son; and now, I can see that it can happen with us too."

Her face was blank but she nodded in agreement.

I turned sideways in my seat and faced her, "Look at it this way; the prodigal son was miserable where he was, but he was happy where he used to be, you know, when he lived at home. The problem was that he felt committed to all the mistakes he already made, and so he just kept on going. Just like us, he kept on making more mistakes because he felt committed to go the way he was going. But one day he just said, *you know what? I change my mind*.

"Huh?"

"That's it. He just said he was going to change his mind and go back to what he had when he was happy."

Britney's eyes opened wide as if to say, "Ok…and so?"

"You see, it wasn't any bigger than just changing his mind. And we can too. We don't have to keep falling deeper into this mess. We can just say *we change our mind* and we can go do something else."

It looked like she got it. Her face brightened and she said, "Ok let's go…right now."

"We will." I smiled.

"No. I mean right now. This minute right now, let's go."

"I got to wait for Rocky. I got to get my money and I got to get my car and get rid of this one."

"Let's go get the Saab."

"Britney? What's up? I told you, we need to get our money."

"You're not going to get any money. They're setting you up."

"Oh bull, why would Rocky do that to me?"

"So they wouldn't have to pay you what they owe you. C'mon let's just do what you said."

"It's not his money. Rocky is doing me a favor."

She surprised me by blurting out an 'almost confession', "Tony told me they were going to set you up." This statement was telling on her. It got my full attention.

I remembered her telling me about a Tony that passed her a note with his number on it once. "You mean that guy that you said hit up on you?"

"Yeah, that's Tony. I ran into him a couple times after that. He ought to know what Rocky has planned. He told me he was going to set you up. That's Rocky's nephew."

"His nephew?"

"Yeah, he said that the two of you were going to butt heads."

"The two of us? Tony and me? Because of you?"

"No. Tony said that you were out to get him and so you would have to butt heads some day."

"I don't even know him...why would I..." I stopped talking and looked at Britney. "Britney, what does Tony do, you know for a living?"

"We only got together a couple of times...that's all. You were mad at me anyway."

"Forget about that. What does this guy do for a living?"

"He's a mechanic."

I nodded my head, "So he's a mechanic and I guess they call him Hot Rod?"

"Yeah," Britney smiled broadly, "That's him. How did you know?"

"Start the car. Let's get out of here."

We crossed over the freeway and were getting ready to use the on-ramp to I-285 when I saw Billy and his girl and someone I didn't recognize coming towards us in my black Subaru. They saw us and pulled into the gas station across from the on ramp we were approaching.

Billy motioned to us and yelled out the window, "Hurry man, c'mon switch cars."

I didn't care whether they had my money from Rocky or not. I had hidden $1500 in my spare tire in the trunk and that's what I wanted. I wanted to get as far away from this part of town as I could. I didn't care who owed who anything, I just wanted to get away, and stay away, and the $1500 and my own car would help. Instead of taking the left onto the freeway I told Britney to pull into the gas station.

She cut back across the road and pulled into the gas station and pulled up facing Billie in my Subaru. Before we could get out of the car two Dekalb County police vehicles were speeding around the curve that Billy just came around. They started to pass us and go over the freeway but Billy honked the horn and switched the headlights back and forth from high to low beams. The cops slammed on their brakes and fishtailed into the station.

I yelled at Britney, "Go...Go..." and I tried to grab the steering wheel and turn it towards the exit but Britney kept her foot on the brake.

She yelled back, "We can't outrun them."

"Go Britney, I mean it, go."

"No. We can't do it."

"It doesn't matter, if we just get around a curve I'll jump out and hit the woods. I can make it."

"Naw, we can't make it." She put both feet on the brake and wrestled me for the steering wheel She knew we could have made it to some point where I would be able to jump out and make it through the woods.

But here was the opportunity she's been waiting for; I was a split second away from having her switch to my side but in front of the others she went along with what she wanted to do all along. She wanted the cops to catch me without me knowing she was the one making it happen.

I yelled, "Come on…. Britney, come on." In the next the moment I fell apart inside and wanted to whine, "Pull-eeze Britney, oh please, please don't do this to me."

Britney has seen me question many things about my personal life, my family life, my financial life, my spiritual life, my sex life; she has even seen me cry. So, now that I feel so lost, so weak, so impudent…why not whine.

Why not? Because at this exact moment I was a new creature. Possible a prayer was being answered, or a mercy given or a change of something…something very special was happening to me and I let out a breath of air, my shoulders dropped and a slight smile relaxed my face.

I often wondered exactly how I would face death. What would I do? How would I act knowing that my life would be over? Getting caught and going to jail was certain death for me. I used to wonder, that when a time like this came, would I whine.

The wondering was over. I looked my disaster in the face and I took it. Just knowing that I could take death, the worst that life could deal me, a tremendous feeling of peace overwhelmed me. There would be no whining.

Our car came to a stop and all the activity outside of the car seemed to be miles away. People were moving and talking and shouting but I heard nothing but a muffled silence. A police officer's hand reached in the car past Britney's head and grabbed the keys and pulled them from the ignition. His hand went back out of the car in slow motion and I watched my escape leaving in his hand. I watched this happen within an arms length away, and it happened so slow that I could have grabbed the keys back, but I didn't.

As he drew his arm back out the window he bent down and looked at me through the open window and said something. A muffled sound, as if it came from a long distance off, may have said, "Keep your hands where I can see them", or maybe it was, "Step out of the car." The words were coming at me from so far away. I waited for them to reach me but by the time they did, each word fell apart and faded. They faded so fast that by the time they got to me, I couldn't make out what they said.

The only thing I heard sounded like a deep down laugh that must have been made by the people who knew the person I chose to trust. I felt shamed and embarrassed. I could only look into Britney's face; she said nothing.

She sat and smiled at me.

I knew why she was smiling.

It was clear to me and I didn't have to pretend any longer that it wasn't.

I knew it was her trying to nail me all along, but it didn't matter anymore. I no longer cared whether I got caught or not. So, in those few minutes that we were facing each other, I had no idea what kind of look was on my face. I may have been smiling too, because her smile grew brighter as we sat there.

I could see no malice in the smile she was giving me. The look on my face must have been one of surprise, mixed with the expectation that everything would fall into place, the way I always knew it should. Inside I was sad, extremely sad, but all I could do was smile.

The good news was…I don't have to run anymore.

The better news was…I didn't kill anyone.

On the other hand, the things that shouldn't have mattered at all, is what hurt the most: The officer opened the door for Britney, "Are you alright?" He reached her arm with his left hand and helped her out of the car. His right hand was down along his right leg and I knew that's where he would be holding his gun. His eyes never left me as he helped Britney out of the car.

It mattered to me that she was getting such the royal treatment while I was being hunted as if I were a mass murderer. She's in this with me, why are they treating her like gold?

It mattered to me that the young guy sitting on the hood of my Subaru put his arms around Britney as they watched me get out of the car at gunpoint to get handcuffed and placed in the cop's car.

It mattered to me that their empty faces held nothing but the curiosity of watching each step of the process unfold, swallow me up, and then fold back again.

What mattered most was accepting, once and for all, that the one person I always thought was on my side was always against me.

And now, I visualized myself walking through a dimly lit tunnel that led away from the crowd. The concrete walk sloped down and echoed the sound of one set of cleats walking down into the dark shadow of the silent stillness ahead of me and away from an arena filled with life and action.

An intense feeling of aloneness gripped me, as if I was being removed from an important game, while everyone else continued to play.

I saw myself being extracted from life and carried to another world. I went into dark tunnels, and out again, and then into deeper and darker ones, as I was carried further away from life. Then after going through one razor-wired gate after another we reached a loading dock where people were being processed and booked for crimes against the state.

When I got out of the squad car the floating fantasy was shattered by the clatter of reality, noise, and lighted rooms. Aside from an isolated burst of profanity, and screaming that erupted occasionally, from an over crowded cell down a sterile hallway, hollow people sat quietly staring through vacant eyes as they waited to be locked away.

I was checked in, fingerprinted, photographed, de-liced, showered, given an orange jumpsuit and bedded down.

In the morning I woke up to a new world and a new way to do everything, but I wasn't feeling down or depressed. I felt comfortable, and actually relieved, that the way I was living was over. At least, at no time did I hear any officer mention the word "homicide" when making reference to the charges against me. Nor were we anywhere near Jackson Lake.

I didn't kill anybody and the best I could figure, those cops I ticked off lost their chance at killing me.

I was a happy camper.

On every ID photo taken of me in jail I was smiling. I joked and laughed with the intake officers and enjoyed looking at the force that would make my life change. When I took the money to kill San Ji, I asked God to do what He had to do to make sure I did the right thing, and this was it.

Getting arrested was the answer to my prayer.

"And he came to himself," the prodigal son went from a pig pen to his father's house when he "came to himself". What the lost son did physically in that story I did spiritually. I was living in a pig sty before I came to this dirty cell but now I was on my way to the Father's house. I may have failed as a bad guy but God succeeded in getting through to me. I may have been lost, but now I had a chance to find where I should be. I may be uncomfortable now, and will probably be treated unfairly in the months or years to come, but I didn't kill anyone.

This could be my 'starting-over' point. I could start over from here

I was surprised to hear at my arraignment that I was charged with two armed robberies that I didn't commit. The first one I knew about but, for the second armed robbery, I was told that I put a gun to Billie's head and took his car. They had a dozen witnesses to backup the charges and my wife hid away and refused to come to my defense.

If I was found guilty on both counts of armed robbery and if the sentences did not run concurrently, the minimum time I would spend in prison would be twenty-years, but if it went passed the minimum I had the possibility of doing life. There was no bond set for my charges. I would have to wait it out a preliminary hearing for the judge to see if there was enough evidence to go to court at all.

That could happen at anytime…in the next year, or two.

27

In the first moments before waking I let my mind wander as I kept my eyes shut. I didn't want to open them and see proof of what I was trying to push away from knowing was true.

Half of me wanted to distract my fears with trying to remember if there was anything I promised to do for anyone or if there was any place special I had to go today. That part of me was lost in the thought that I may need to jump up and rush off someplace. I hoped not to remember anything that would keep me from rolling over and going back to sleep. But just the same I lay in bed trying to think what I may have committed myself to do this morning and so I held my eyes tightly shut as if opening them would wake me more than I wanted to be at the time.

I started gathering my senses when I felt the hardness of the iron bed beneath me. I became more aware of where this recollection was leading me when I sensed the smell of concrete and stainless steel. I heard the sound of voices echoing off in the distance and it all was coming back to me now

Hasn't it happened in every ones life?

Hasn't everyone felt that sudden dread the moment something awful is remembered that happened to them in their life? There's a minute or two of feeling just great when first waking up that gets shattered when suddenly remembering a wrecked car or a broken relationship, or some other painful act that strikes with a sickening feeling.

The feeling is that of hopelessness because it is sensing an act that is over. The feeling is one of being painfully aware of an action that is finished and cannot be changed, a catastrophic and irreversible act. The only thing to be done with a feeling like that is to watch the consequences of the act, you're trying to forget, play out its part and hope the repercussions don't swallow you whole.

Opening my eyes I stared at the words I printed on a sheet of paper and glued with toothpaste to a spot above my bed on the back of the bunk above me. I read the words slowly to myself, "This, too, shall pass."

That thought quickly vanished with the announcement of breakfast: *"Trays Up"* was shouted into the PA system and then came the sound of metal bolts being released in the locks that started with the cells furthest down the 'block' and growing louder as they approached my cell.

The sound of the electronic locks popping open was unmistakably my cue to accept the need to switch my thinking and alter the expectations I had for this day. I opened my eyes to the fact that I wasn't going to be rushing off anywhere special today.

Quickly rapping on the bottom of the bunk above me, I said, "C'mon Ray...I think its scrambled eggs today. Rise and shine man."

"Sell my tray for a Moon Pie and two chips." Ray answered and rolled over.

I countered with, "A Moon Pie and *one* chip."

"Take a flying leap, Mr. Rick Flair." Ray said as he jumped off the top rack. "You know they gonna have sausage and probably flapjacks too. You a fool trying to gyp me down."

I was given the nickname Rick Flair at four different facilities I was in, all independent of each other, and I never referred to myself by that name. I have never seen Rick Flair so I don't know what anyone is branding me as. But I do like the name and I heard he was a wrestler, so I didn't mind the reference.

"Well *Mister* Ray, you're the one who's too lazy to get up and eat but the difference of one bag of chips sure changed your mind."

The cell door opened and I walked out into the "day" room.

The day room was half the size of a basketball court surrounded by twenty-foot high concrete walls. Over one wall opposite the two-story row of cells was an observation glass. It was a thick one-way glass with guards on the other side in a control booth.

The day room was empty except for five steel picnic tables and steel benches bolted to the floor. There was a television set on a wall mount and a row of four pay phones across the room from the TV.

In the middle of one of the sidewalls was a common toilet and was to be used by any of the inmates not in their cell since the cells were locked anytime the prisoners were in the day room. The inmates were out of their cells two hours in the morning and two hours in the afternoon. The other twenty hours a day we were locked down.

I walked over to the row of phones and took off my shoe and placed the phone's receiver inside my shoe and placed it on the metal stool in front of the phone. The phones wouldn't be turned on until seven o'clock but I just reserved a first call on one.

The doors swung open and two trustees pushed the huge cart of breakfast trays into the day room.

I climbed the stairs to get at the end of the line.

Someone yelled, "Sausage for milk."

"You're covered."

A different voice yelled, "Sausage for eggs."

No reply.

Then a familiar voice yelled, "Breakfast tray for a moon pie and two chips."

I yelled back, "A moon pie and one chip."

"Shut up Rick Flair," the voice yelled back.

"Come on Ray...no one's going to go a moon pie and two chips."

A voice from the middle of the line yelled, "I'll go with it."

Ray answered, "You're on...but I keep the milk."

The voice yelled, "Naw man...the milk goes with the tray."

"OK...but I keep the bread," said Ray.

The voice yelled, "OK Ray...and I'll keep the moon pie and two chips."

Ray yelled back, "OK...a moon pie and one chip and I keep the milk."

No reply.

I yelled, "Hey Ray, a moon pie and one chip for your tray."

There were no more bids. Ray said, "Go ahead cheap skate...a moon pie and one chip and I keep the..."

"I get the tray Ray...the whole tray."

"OK," Ray said, "Don't be so touchy."

In the months that dragged by, we got out of our cells a couple hours in the morning, and a couple hours in the afternoon. Twenty hours of every day was spent sharing an 8x10 cell with another inmate. The time out of the cell was spent in the "day room" with about thirty other prisoners. I met a man who was a preacher on the outside and I adopted him as my "spiritual leader". His name was Herb and he would hold prayer meetings and bible studies for those of us getting into the Word.

Herb may have been my spiritual leader but I was far from his spiritual pupil. As a matter of fact, I got the distinct feeling that Herb couldn't stand me. Because in the talks we would have about the bible, I constantly attacked the people he told me were supposed to be so great in the bible.

Moses was a murderer and David was even worse. Abraham said his wife was his sister to protect himself and Sarah was put into the Pharaohs harem. Jacob was a con man, Noah got drunk and as a result, a whole people became cursed. I couldn't see what was so good about any of them. How could any of them make it in the "good" book? And I had to live the rest of my life in prison?

I never was able to manipulate the truth to be what I wanted it to be but it seemed all these characters always had something that made people just forget the bad they did, and yet, I'm going to die in prison for doing much less than what any of them did.

Unless, of course, I can get into this biblical favor somehow.

I sat down, "Hey Herb, I have a great idea."

"Oh really?" Herb didn't look up from his plate. He was never excited about the great ideas I came up with. "What's it this time?"

"I'm going to work for the Lord."

That got Herbs attention, "That's good. As a matter of fact, that's *real* good." Herb was happy to hear this type of commitment coming from me. He quit eating, put down his fork and said, "It was just a matter of time Duke. I prayed that you would come around."

"Well, I've finally decided."

Herb was genuinely happy for me. I could see it in his smile.

I leaned forward on my elbows, "This is what I am going to do. I'm going to make a deal with God. I am going to promise him that when I get out of here I will enter the ministry and I'll become a preacher." I smiled broadly, "What do you think of that?"

The happy look on Herb's face dropped to disbelief, "What?"

"I'm serious man. I'm really going to do it. I'm going to start working for God. I'm going to get into the Word and help people who are hurting. I'll come back here and tell these guys how I used to be and now I'm better. And I'll tell everybody how I got myself out of this mess."

The furrows over Herb's eyes were deeply formed into a scowl, "You're going to what?"

"Yep."

Herb yelled, "You phony."

"What's wrong with you? I will. Really I will, I'll work for the Lord. You watch, when I get out of here I'll…"

Herb picked up his fork and started eating again, "Do you know how stupid you sound?"

I didn't answer but I'm sure my blank face covered the question well.

Herb kept eating as he talked, "You're a phony! Number One: you don't make deals with God; and another thing if you were going to work for him out there you could work for him in here. There are more people in here who need God's help and there are more people in here who would listen. You don't want to work for God; you just want to get out of your troubles. You're a liar and a phony." Herb picked up his tray and moved to another table.

I thought it was a good plan and I couldn't understand why Herb was getting so mad at me. I figured he must be having a bad day or something, but I couldn't worry about that right now…Harold got out yesterday.

Harold had been waiting to go to court for three months and he went to court yesterday. It was just a preliminary hearing to see if they would hold him over for superior court and the witness that filed the charges against him didn't come to court. I've had dozens of those kinds of cases. The judge had to throw it out for lack of evidence. If no one's there to testify against you, there's no case against you and the judge can't do anything else but throw it out.

In Georgia, if anyone wanted to have you arrested, all they would have to do would be to have a friend be a false witness and pay $35 for the cost of the warrant and have you thrown in jail. Once you're arrested you can't file a cross warrant or even deny the validity of the one against you. The only thing you can do is go to jail, be arraigned, bail yourself out if a bond is set, hire an attorney, and then show up in court.

The other side doesn't have to do a thing but pay $35 and a lie to put one more nail in your coffin.

Harold went to court yesterday and when they brought him back to his cell he hardly had time to sit down before a guard yelled, "Harold Bartley, bag and baggage."

Today, I was finally going to get my day in court, and as much as I hate to do it, I needed to call Britney and remind her to come to court. The evidence against me was false but she was the only one who could confirm my story. Bottom line though, I was counting on a "Harold Bartley Day" and have the charges dropped because of the witnesses not appearing in court.

I dialed Britney's number and as the phone rang I was afraid she might not still live there, but when she answered, I realized I was really hoping she didn't. It hurt talking to her but it hurt more to have to ask something of her, "Britney, my hearing is today. You need to be in court in Decatur at 10 O'clock this morning."

There was no answer.

"Did you hear me?"

I heard some muffled sounds.

"Britney, hello Britney…do you hear me? I need you to be there for me, you are my only witness."

After a long silence she spoke softly, "You're not ever getting out; you know that, don't you?" And then she laughed and I heard someone else laugh with her.

"Britney, what are you doing?"

"I'm in bed baby, getting something you never gave me."

"What do you mean by…" I heard the other voice again, "who's that?"

She laughed, "Tony…silly." There was more laughter.

No anger…no sadness…just a terrible ripping in my gut. I quietly hung the phone up as they both laughed.

I sat for a few blank moments assessing the damage I felt. Surprisingly enough, I was Ok. I thought I would freak out like many of the guys do when they get through with a call like that.

I looked over at Herb but he wouldn't look my way. I sure wish I knew what I said wrong that got him mad.

After breakfast the next piece of excitement for the day would be exchanging the sheets for clean ones. That would happen around noon and everyone looked forward to it. After that, we sat in an 8x10 cell and did nothing.

Tomorrow morning we would place our underwear and socks and towel in a pile to be washed and returned in the afternoon. That would be the activity for the day. It would only take 3 or 4 minutes but we all looked forward to it because after that, we sat and did nothing.

The next day around 11am everyone lined up at the door and exchanged our soiled uniforms for clean ones and that would be the activity for the day and we looked forward to it. More nothing.

On Fridays we made an order to receive junk food and incidentals from the store, if we had any money on the books. We could buy candy bars, potato chips, moon pies, pads of paper, toothpaste, a comb. We're able to order a number of things I used to take for granted, that is; if we had any money on the books. That would be the activity of the day and we looked forward to it and then to more nothing.

On Tuesdays our orders come in and we definitely looked forward to that. The "nothing" we did on those days were filled with a bit more "something."

This was the routine day after day, week after week, and month after month as I waited to go to a prison and do this routine for the rest of my life. Those few minutes on any day that differed from those few minutes on another day were the only thing that broke up our time. Of course we went to church service or AA or anything that got us out of the cell for a while. Because 20 hours a day of sitting on an iron bed every day of the week, every week of the month, and every month of the year was a killer. It was this forced waste of life that punished me for the deliberate waste of life that put me here.

Something in me refused to accept any more waste. I took to reading the bible. I set a goal of reading a certain number of pages each day and then muscled through the reading. The hardest part was the, so and so begat so and so, and on and on. But I muscled through it. I doubt that I understood what I read but I got it behind me, just so I'd be able to say some day, "I read the bible…cover to cover."

So, for the most part, reading the bible was not much more than looking at each word. But it grew from that point to be more than that. In some spots I got into the story and grew curious about what I just read. When I asked Herb about those spots, he explained them in a way that allowed me to know more about my life, just by knowing more about the meaning of those stories in the bible.

I was starting to understand why anyone would seriously want to study the bible.

The PA system announced a list of names, mine included, of people who need to line up at the door to be bused over to the court house.

"Hey Ray, get my sheets for me will you. I'm going to court."

"It'll cost you."

"Whatever Ray, what goes around comes around."

"Oh, Rick…chill man, you know I'll take care of it."

After the long ordeal of getting transported to the court house with 30 other inmates it was finally my turn to go in front of the judge. As I walked into the court room I was thinking that I might be all wrong about Britney because surely she knew how serious this was. Who would condemn anyone to a life in prison just to own what little I have? Surely she would be in the court room waiting to tell the judge what really happened and I'd be able to go home just like all the other times.

Whenever anyone swore out a phony warrant against me in the past, no one from that side showed up in court, and so it disturbed me to see Billy and his wife. Billy was driving my car when they led the cops to me the night I was arrested. I don't know why but I smiled and waved. Billy's wife smiled back and Billy waved and immediately my fear switched to hope again

Then I saw Rocky and three other people I never saw before and they all sat together in one pocket on that side of the court room and all hope went south.

When the Judge called my case they all rose and moved to a table to the right of the table where I was sitting. The arresting officer by regulation sits on the side of the prosecution and so the scene looked to be overwhelming lopsided against me.

The public defender sat with me on our side of the courtroom. But I kept watching the door thinking that any moment Britney would come to my rescue. But she never did.

The judge felt that since I was arrested thirty times in the last few years and was never convicted that I was finding my way around the law. And now he was excited, and eager, to put me away for anything that he could make stick.

As he heard witness after witness say that I put a gun to Billy's head and took his car the judge actually laughed and said, "This will be interesting. I'm looking forward to watching this one myself. The only question here will be how much time over the minimum we'll be able to give you."

My life was over.

28

The judge determined that there was ample evidence to hold the case over and setting a bond was out of the question. My next hearing could be months down the line, it could even be years before I get back to court. I don't have an attorney and everyone from whom I asked for help had turned me down.

The case against me was just too strong.

There wasn't anything that could be done.

I got Herb to start speaking to me again and I continued to blitz read the bible and with Herb's help I even started understanding some of it.

Herb made it sound interesting. As a matter of fact, he would get so excited himself as he explained things, that he got me excited too. He would show me something in the bible and then say, "Ok now, turn to…" and he would take me to another place in the bible and point to the verse and say, "Now SEE THAT…huh? See it…" and he would get up and pace back and forth as he repeated, "See what's going on…isn't that something…" and then he would quickly sit down again and say, "Now, let's go deeper, let me show you this. Turn to the book of…" and he kept revealing one mystery after another.

I could actually see what it was that he was showing me. I saw what was exciting Herb because it was all starting to make sense to me. I began to understand the message in some of the words that I blitzed read. I started to see the beautiful story of Jesus and I saw the coming of Jesus early on in the Old Testament and then I saw how the prophecy fell into place. The one thing I needed to know now was; *how will any of this help me get out of here?*

I wanted to know how I could *use* what I was coming to understand about the bible. I made a point to spend as much time as I could with Herb in the four hours we were out of our cells and I studied the bible the other twenty hours that I wasn't sleeping when I was locked down.

Several days, I chose to stay locked down during the time in the morning and the night that we could go out into the day room. When I was alone in my cell I continued, week after week, trying to get the words out that I made for my prayer.

I failed.

The words would get stuck.

I literally could not say the words Herb was leading me to say. I couldn't say that I would gladly work for the Lord even if I had to stay in prison. I kept trying to say that prayer, but it always ended the same, "But Lord, why can't I get out of here? You know I'm not guilty of what they're charging me. Once they send me to prison, at my age, my life will be over…please let me out of here."

This was the only thing I could focus on; asking God to get me out.

The months went by and my daughter Tracy would visit me from time to time and Cynthia would put money on the books in a duty bound kindness to a father she had no time to visit. My son did neither, he didn't help put anything on the books for me, and he didn't visit, nor did he write. No one wrote.

Ray had been in this jail a long time. He had been incarcerated for five years and in county for three years. Since he was battling his case in court he got his attorney to keep him in county for that entire time.

I didn't ask any questions about his crime, but I did ask him this, "Ray you've been away from your friends and family for eight years now but someone visits you nearly every day. How do you do it? I write my kids and say things that I think would get them here but my one daughter is the only one who comes and that hasn't been but a few times. But you, it doesn't fail. Every day your family visits you."

"Oh it isn't every one, they all take turns. They have pretty much set up a schedule on which days they come."

"I still don't understand it. How do you get them to come, and then, how do you keep them coming every day, year after year?"

Ray jumped down from his bunk as if this was an important thing he wanted to tell me. "Duke, I don't do anything *now*. There's nothing I *can* do. I'm not making any money; I can't take them out somewhere. I can't bring my wife flowers or take my kids to the ball game. I never thought of it before, but I can see it now."

"What?"

"It's an investment, man. When I was out of here, and when I was at home, I gave my family a great deal of love and attention. I went to all my kid's functions, ball games, scout meetings, birthday parties…oh, I didn't know the investment part of what I was doing, but I was making deposits then into the account I'm drawing from now. I wanted to be there, you know…to spend time with them. I guess now they just want to be here with me."

I didn't say anything. There was nothing I could say.

Ray said, "I didn't know I was building an *emotional* bank account that I would be drawing out of some day. I was just *loving* my family. Now, they're just *loving* me." Ray jumped back up on his bunk and laid down facing the wall and said, "I guess that's all I ever done that was right."

"I guess that was enough though…huh?"

He was asleep. That fast, he was asleep.

Punishment, I thought, this was the punishment. Everything someone said in here was for the purpose of punishment. To know what I should do, now that it's impossible to do it, and now, to know what I didn't do…that's the punishment.

I sat on my bunk and began my prayers again, "Dear Lord, get me out of here. Get me out so I can show my kids I love them. Let me start making deposits in their lives." I probably wasn't doing it right but I cut straight to the point because evidently, God didn't know what it was I needed.

I failed to show my children I loved them when I had the chance and now I'll never get the chance. When they needed me, I failed them and now I'll probably die before I have another chance to show that I loved them. It wasn't that I didn't love my children it was that I was too selfish to learn how to show it. What an unfair thing this is. Why punish them? Why take me out of the picture now that I know better?

I whispered to myself, "I do love them, don't I?"

God shrugged and whispered back, "Love is what love does."

29

In the afternoon, a sandwich with meat turning green and a bit rancid was handed through the slot in our cell door along with a small bag of chips and a cookie. We ate the meat with the cookie because we saved the bread for Dillard down in 401. We always saved oranges and packets of sugar and especially the bread to contribute towards the booze they made in 401. If we got enough ingredients to him, before any of the house busts, we would all share in some jail house hooch. It didn't taste all that bad and it didn't get you all that drunk but it gave us a good buzz and we did it more for the deviousness of doing what we weren't suppose to do.

Once or twice a month, the door of the day room would fly open and a dozen cops in head gear and face shields, batons and rubber gloves would come running through the door screaming.

All the lock bolts on the cells would pop open at the same time and the cops would yell at us, "Out...down...Out...down "as they threw us out of our cells. The cops that stayed out to watch us yelled for us to get down and the others ran into our cells and started throwing out bedding, and whatever else we had in our cell. If we gathered anything over time, it was considered "contraband" and that was thrown out the door. If we had two pencils, the second was contraband and was thrown into the middle of the dayroom floor and later swept and bagged by a trustee.

Of course, anything we were not "supposed" to have is called contraband and it's confiscated. That would include the tray I made with an old paper bag. I pressed tiny folds down the sides and hardened it with a piece of soap. I used the tray to hold my extra packets of mustard and catsup and salt and pepper. But that was "contraband" and it was thrown in the pile in the middle of the floor. I also had three pads of paper on which I had written personal notes and poetry. That was considered excessive paper and therefore contraband. Months of recording what I thought to be magnificent insights that I was sure would never come my way again, thrown in the pile in the middle of the room and later tossed in the garbage.

After that, I began to mail my notes to my daughter as letters. I wrote in great lengths on things I had hoped would explain why I lived my life the way I did. My explanations added up to nothing more than a dysfunctional pile of excuses, that would have been better off tossed in the middle of the room, with the rest of the garbage, but instead, they were disguised as well-meaning letters and sent to my daughter.

It was as if I were asking to have the effects of my flaws be removed without actually removing them. I wanted to be forgiven purely on the basis that I was hurting and scared.

Hurting and scared! Now, when I think of the phrase "hurting and scared" I see something quite a bit different. Today I can look back and see a twelve year old little girl turning a corner of her life and crossing an important mile stone as she becomes a teenager. What an opportunity for a father to grab this moment in his daughter's life and use it to help mold her character for her future. I remember how my youngest daughter looked up to me. I remember the games we played at night when I put her to bed. I would lie down and start to read her a story and pretend to fall asleep and then, start snoring real loud. She would start tickling me and then I would tickle her back until it turned into a wrestling match.

We always ended up playing a card game of Gin-Rummy. I would let her win her next day's spending money, and then we would both fall asleep.

I worked late at my karate school each night and so every night when I got home the cards would already be shuffled and our "hands" would be dealt on the foot of the bed and we would play our game of cards as soon as I came in. After she would win her money I would tell her a scary story that I made up, and before I ever finished the story we would end up laughing, giggling, wrestling, and then, like the night before, and the one before that, we would both fall asleep.

One night she shuffled the cards and dealt us both a hand and waited for me to come home. But, she fell asleep waiting for me, and when her mother came in the next morning, there my daughter lay, all by herself, with the cards all dealt out and un-played. The next night she shuffled and dealt the cards again, and then the next night, and the night after that one. But each morning, her mother found that she fell asleep waiting for me to come home.

But, I didn't come home.

I never thought of the little heart that waited for me to return each night, the love that was being missed, the guidance, the support, and the father I took away from her.

To be perfectly frank, the lesson I was learning back then in jail, about being scared and hurt, wasn't coming through the way it's coming to me now. At that time, I didn't remember that I was always too busy to spend time with Tracy. I didn't remember that I was so full of myself that I belittled my son Derek, because he didn't live up to being the athlete I never was.

Nor, did I remember my life was too full of wild and reckless pleasures, when Cynthia needed my support. Even after it was pointed out to me in so many ways, I was still able to sweep it aside and scream, *me-me-me* in my own head as I questioned, "Why are you all ignoring me? Can't you see I'm hurting?"

I was even hurt when I was to learn later that my daughter never opened my notes I sent to her as 'letters' and they were never read and my self-absorbed excuses ended up being thrown away anyway.

I'm glad she didn't open those letters. There is no use in trying to explain things after the fact, or to make deposits in an account that had been closed, or had gone bankrupt. There are some things that just do not fall in the category of "it is never too late".

Don't believe the statement, "it is never too late." Take it from me, when the bus has pulled away from the station and you're not on it…it *is* too late.

That doesn't mean you can't go on from where you are. There will be other buses and maybe you can take a train, a plane, or walk. But to catch a ride on that bus you were hoping for…when it leaves without you…it *is* too late. It's not coming back to pick you up or to make things right. Nothing does good but good itself.

Don't expect to draw on accounts where no deposits were made. It's too late for that. The only thing "never too late" means is you can start making deposits at any time. Even if it's too late to make withdrawals, it is never too late to make deposits.

My train of thought was interrupted, "UUR...RRCH, NOW" The PA system screeched a command. The system worked Ok but the guards didn't know how to use it. They put the microphone too close to their mouth and it was always hard to tell what they were saying. If you've been there long enough you could tell what was being said purely out of the habit of the schedule and this was church night.

"Ray, what was that last thing he said?"

"He said its church service, man. Can't you understand English, come on let's go get God in us."

Ray pounded on our cell door to get the attention of the guard in the tower and he popped our lock.

I said, "Anything to get out of this hole for a while."

A few people from each block joined together at the service and that gave us a chance to see a new face or two. But what really amazed me was to look at that man standing in the front of the room talking to us about Jesus and God and the Holy Spirit and to think that when he leaves us he is going to go home. It was so hard for me to comprehend that the man standing right there in front of me is just going to walk out of here. The doors are going to open for him right on cue just as he expects them to, and he will just walk through them.

It was hard for me to think how wonderful that would feel.

I wanted to shake his hand before he left. It just made me feel good to shake the hand of someone who was truly free. And, to me, being truly free was being outside walking on that sidewalk, eight floors down.

Of course the guards go out of here too but I don't see them as 'people' and we certainly don't shake their hand. They were a part of the system and I could see how miserable they were in the miserable way they treated us. They were just as much a prisoner in here as we were.

But the preacher-man, he was a civilian. He could choose when to come back and he could even decide not to come back at all if he wanted, but the guards; they were prisoners to this system just like me.

There was something magical to see a man stand in front of me who could walk into Steak and Shake and order a double cheeseburger and a Vanilla Milkshake if he wanted. And if he never wanted to come back in here he didn't have to, now, that was power. It must be power coming from God.

I couldn't deaden myself to myself and sleep my time away. Some people did just that, they slept for extremely long periods of time all the time. But for me. My time behind bars was filled with reflection of what I was all about and where it got me and I even understood, to some degree, that there was something very special happening in me as I began to understand what other people meant to me.

It all had something to do with God. I just didn't know what that was.

There were days that being in jail was the most exact place in life that I could be, and it was on those days, that I was glad I was there to receive what I was being taught.

Such a costly time, this time spent in here. But it was a valuable time as well, if you let it be. I didn't want it to be a waste of life, so I tried to find some lesson that might offset the price I had to pay for it. I'm not romancing the thought of having been there. But it was better than killing someone, and probably the most right thing for my life at the time. But there were so many times that I felt my time had passed and I wanted out so bad it literally doubled me over with a pain in the gut.

"Hey, I learned my lesson…now, let me go."

It doesn't work that way. Once you learn your lesson you just break even. The price you have to pay is the *waste of your life* beyond the break even point.

I was still in the state of wonderment of the preacher type people choosing to come in here and spend their golden moments with us. The time itself must have certainly been the "golden" moments in their life because it was *their* time. How they used that time wasn't decided by a paycheck or by an obligation to be fulfilled. It was the time in their life that they owned as their very own. It was the time they spent with a perfectly free choice of how to use it, and they chose to spend with us.

One night an old man in his eighties came by our pod to give us his golden moments. Our small cell blocks were housed in what was known as a "pod". If you were outside of the cell block, and in the hallway, you could walk in a circle and pass all eight doors to the eight cell blocks in the pod. In the center of that circle was the control center that was elevated so the guards could keep watch on each of the eight sections in that circle that made up the pod.

The old man who came by every week looked to be about six foot four and wore a red plaid shirt and a pair of jeans. He went from one section to another in a circle around the pod. He looked like an older version of the Marlboro man but instead of a horse, he carried a chair. He carried it from the door of one block of cells to the next. He also carried a stack of magazines and when he got to one door he would open the 1x2 ft metal slot below the clear Plexiglas, that was the upper half of the door, and sit with his shoulders stooped over and wait until someone came to the door.

Sometimes, several men would go to the door and bunch around to see what magazines he had; and at other times, no one would come at all. He would sit and wait for a period of time before closing up the metal slot and picking up his chair and going to the door of the next cell block and repeat the process.

The day I met him no one else came to the door. He sat and waited for what seemed to be a long time, but no one came. The look of kindness and compassion on his face drew me to the door, "What'cha got?" I asked.

His huge wrinkled hands shook with age as he began to thumb through the few magazines he had. They were outdated Sunday school pamphlets and other used bible tracts and I sat down and looked through the slot but didn't see anything that I would want to read. There wasn't a lot to offer in the way of what I thought would be interesting to read but I quickly saw that handing out those magazines wasn't the only reason he was there. He leaned forward and in a low husky voice said, "I want to say a prayer for you?"

I thought he meant he'd like to pray for me sometime, maybe some night before he went to bed, or whenever people who pray, actually do it, and so I said, "Ok."

He surprised me because, right there and then, he reached a big wrinkled hand through the opening and I sat there staring at this huge wrinkled hand shaking. Not knowing anything else to do, I grabbed his hand, and he began to pray. I don't remember the prayer but I remember him. It was after his prayer that I realized that although I wasn't guilty for the crime that was taking my life from me; I was guilty for the life I agreed to take from someone else. I was guilty of wasting the precious life God gave me doing the things I was doing. But more than anything else I was guilty of turning my back and moving my life away from God.

As this old man prayed for me I became thankful to Rocky and to the witnesses who lied against me. I started to understand how glad I was to be arrested because it kept me from doing what I had set out to do. I remembered about the time that I prayed that God would make something happen that would get me off the course that I was on. And with that in mind I began believing in the power of prayer.

I thought about the old man that visited us in "B" pod and prayed with me. I wondered if he was here one day or some place like it. Did he return here so that he could invest into accounts where deposits in his past were never made?

The questions were there but the answers didn't really matter all that much. It was important for me to know what the questions were for my life. As for the answers, the old man prayed and the answers were left up to God.

That old man didn't know I once lived in a whore house and later married a prostitute off the street, or that I protected drug dealers, collected for crooks and gamblers, hurt people for profit, and then one night backed my running mate when he shot and killed a drug dealer, and that I, myself, accepted payment to kill someone.

He didn't know a thing about my life and he still prayed for me. I thought that was cool.

Wow, in that case just consider what trust Christ had to have in me. He knows all about me and He hasn't given up on me yet. He knows all about me and He still thought I was worth dying for. He knows something I don't know, something about my life that doesn't show yet. There's something about my life that I'm beginning to understand has a purpose. But before I reach for that purpose I must accept the job of discovering what it is that God knows about me.

I made the decision to get close to God and find out what's going on.

30

I shook the preachers hand and thought of that old man who carried his chair and stopped at the door in front of every block of cells in our "pod"

When I was with that old man the thought of getting out of jail didn't interfere with his prayer, or anything else he said to me. As he prayed for me, I had no thoughts of leaving, or going anywhere. I was at home in his voice and content to be right where I was. I felt so safe listening to the words he spoke and I felt that God heard every thing he said.

Today's preacher talked about anointing and this was a brand new concept to me. I never heard of anything like that. I couldn't wait until I could see Herb again and ask him about this stuff, this anointing. It sounded like something powerful.

Maybe if I could get someone to anoint me, that might be the thing that will get me out of here.

I was getting excited about that prospect of finding something magical that was going to work for me to get me out. I'm glad Herb is teaching me again but I better be careful what I say to him. I seem to get him upset when I tell him how I see the way all these things in the bible can be used to get me out of jail.

When I got back to the pod my cell was in lock down. I walked past the television set on my way to my cell and I saw a familiar face. A movie was playing and I stopped to watch it for a second or two. Carver, the guy I play chess with from 413 pointed to the screen, "Now Rick Flair, there's a guy who could take any of your kicks and give you double back."

The movie he was watching was Lone Wolf McQuade. He was pointing to Chuck Norris. I felt a pain in my gut that traveled up my chest and to my throat. The wrenching in my gut made me sick.

"You think so, Carver?"

Carver was an avid Chuck Norris fan, "I know so…oh yeah, you know who that is don't you? How do you think that karate stuff you do, would do against him? All that kicking the wall in the yard...you know what? The wall, it don't kick back..."

Stewart laughed, "Oh yeah? The wall broke his foot last month. I don't see him kicking the wall around no more."

The "yard" is where we get our outdoor recreation. The outdoors for us was a concrete basketball court on the seventh floor. The concrete walls were three stories high and opened to the sky and the fresh air. It's where the rest of the guys play basketball.

In my first days, when I began my workout program, I stretched and did my karate kicks against the concrete wall. With the tennis shoes I wore the flat rubber soles made a loud sharp popping sound when I timed the distance just right. In the beginning, a couple of the others in the "yard" from our cell block would mock my movements and laugh and then when I started my laps and ran around the court, several of the guys would fall in behind me and be swinging their fists and kicking the air as they laughed and said, "Watch out...I be bad," and then they laughed some more. We had forty in our block in B-Pod and I was the only white person, so I knew there was going to be a challenge.

I usually ignored them as I jogged around the yard, but on one lap when I was feeling especially spirited, I came up to the far wall where I was doing my kicks earlier and jumped up into the air and turned in mid air as my left leg shot out like a piston and struck the wall at just the right distance and made a loud explosive sound. My body continued around and I landed facing the wall, and then I continued running. Everyone who was following me stopped and made like they were *pretending* to be impressed, but I could tell that they really were.

After that day, they never mocked or made fun of me. From that day on they called me Rick Flair...Nature Boy, and the routine I started that day was what I followed. The rest of the guys ignored me as I worked out and they all played basketball at the other end of the court. When I ran laps I had to pass through the basketball court but they never objected.

As a matter of fact, I became such a 'fixture" to the routine, that not only was I ignored as I ran through their play, it became a rule that if the ball hit me it was as if the ball hit the wall and it was ruled out of bounds.

And that was the rules with which we all got along.

One day though, my kicks against the wall were feeling so good I continued increasing the power. I was doing spinning back kicks and when I timed the spin, the thrust, and the re-cock of the foot, the sound off the wall was like an explosion. Finally I jumped up, spun around and fully extended my leg as if the wall would give way as a heavy bag would and hit it with such force I broke my foot.

I took quite a ribbing from the others but it also smoothed off some rough edges between me a few who were less friendly.

"I'll be back out there…It's not all that bad."

"Come on" Carver pointed to the TV.

"Nah, I'm in lock down. You know I don't watch TV."

Would they really believe me if I told them that Chuck Norris was my karate instructor and regular workout partner? Should I tell everyone that he and I were business partners at one time, or that we wrote two books together?

Maybe I should just tell them to watch the credits at the end of the movie and try to guess why my name is up there. But I didn't, I kept my mouth shut. I was ashamed to have been such a dismal failure after having had such great opportunities in life.

I felt sick to my stomach being where I was, and knowing where I could have been.

It was when I got back to my cell and I laid down that I closed my eyes and saw Chuck and me running the bridal paths in Rolling Hills. We talked along the way and it was usually in the conversations we had as we worked out that Chuck delivered messages that would become the foundation on which I would build my life.

I thought of that day when Chuck asked me, "You know what my idea of hell is?"

"What?"

"It would be when, at the end of your life, God comes down and says, *now; let me show you what you could have been.*"

I never heard that statement before that day nor have I heard it since, but I have repeated it enough times that I'll not forget the feeling I had when I first heard Chuck say it to me.

I'm usually aware of the extraordinary value in the message provided by a great thought when I hear it. I'm also experienced at feeling the consequences of ignoring them. It's all the in-between stuff at which I usually fail. I've been slack in the implementation of good thoughts and the discipline to get me where I say I want to be.

Living life by trial and error is painful. It hurt to think of the opportunities and the clear guidance I ignored and so I didn't want to add to the crunch of guilt by watching TV, and see people I knew, in the process of succeeding in their lives.

I couldn't even look out the window and watch the people being successful at staying free to choose where and when they ate, slept, showered, or spent the rest of their day.

Now, my cell was on the seventh floor of a huge, cold gray building that sat on Memorial Drive overlooking the intersection to Interstate freeway 285. I've never thought of any reason to use the word *loomed* before, I never used it for anything else before, but when I saw this building one day from where I stood on Memorial Drive, six blocks away, that's the first word that came to my mind; *loomed.*

And it was not a pretty thought. From Memorial Drive, one could see this massive rock of a building, with slits for windows, *looming* over this small part of the world in Decatur Georgia. It was like Darth Vader's space ship and a feeling of something dark and eerie hovered in my mind, and held me in place, as I looked too long at this massive rock building. I visualized the gray cement being poured over me.

From the inside, of the 18x36 inch slit in the thick stone wall, I could look through the safety glass that kept me from the free fresh air outside. I could see cars going by as if this building wasn't here at all. I wondered if anyone knew of the thousands of lives buried in here.

If only there were bars instead of thick glass I could sneak a message out to some passerby, "Help...I'm being held captive...they're holding me against my will."

"So what" the passerby would say as he crumples my note without looking up at me. "You're getting what you deserve."

I answer back, "Oh well, just a thought."

Those cars didn't have to ignore me as they drove by though; and then, as if to rub it in, they pulled into a Steak and Shake a couple blocks down the street. They knew I could see them from my cell, and so they pulled into the parking lot and leisurely walk inside. They probably order the Steak Burger, Fries, and a Vanilla Shake.

My mouth watered at the thought.

"Hey Ray, the first thing I'm going to do, when I get out of here, is go to Steak and Shake. I'm going to get me a Steak Burger and…"

Ray chimed in, "I know, I know…and fries and a vanilla shake…get away from that window man. You ain't going no where."

Ray was right I needed to move away from the window. I'd get claustrophobic as I get buried in the fantasies of what I long to do when I think of freely walking down that street below. It was exactly that sense of longing that punished me. Seeing what I could have had, thinking of what I could have been, these empty longings created the hollowness in my chest that gave no apparent reason for the next breath I took.

But why breathe at all?

The thought of *not breathing* made vivid to me the fact that I was being slowly smothered from this world. Each day I was hit harder than the day before with the realization that I was buried alive.

31

I never thought of remorse as being thick, or even thin, for that matter. I never really though of remorse, at all. But now, I felt so tightly wrapped with sorrow for the things I had done, remorse was smothering me.

I was truly sorry. Yet, if the truth were known, there was an image that appeared to me, even then, whereby the thickness of my remorse would slice open like a piece of Jell-O if ever the moment came that I had the opportunity to do those things again.

I had very little trust in my *recovery* at this point.

I was ashamed that this pitiful life I lived was so important to me that I would fight to hold on to it. There was remorse for the way I dropped my life into a hole but I was ashamed that I continued to live. I felt it was a great dishonor for me to try and stay alive

Visitors, church services, television and letters were just a taste of what I'll never have again. This taste was just big enough to hurt; that's all. Having a small taste of what you can't have creates the feeling that punishes; knowing what won't ever be mine again, knowing what I'll never do again, knowing what I'll never have again. I had to shrink my world to what I could see within the reach of my own two hands, or end up in the "fishbowl" again.

One day I ripped off my clothes, tore at my face and skin and banged my head against the door as I tried to get out of an interrogation room. I wanted to jump over the second story railing and do a nose dive into the concrete floor below. The harder I tried to get through the door the more desperate I felt. My senses were peaking to a point I could not understand. I finally climbed up on the tiny little table in the small interrogation room and dove to the floor head first. No broken neck. All it did was knock me out.

I was taken away and woke up in the "fishbowl".

The fishbowl was a room with a two-story tall ceiling and was 6 feet wide by 18 feet long. One wall was thick plexi-glass from the floor to the 12 foot ceiling. On my side of this Plexiglas wall was the 6x18 foot totally empty space. On the other side of the Plexiglas was a larger room about 18x18 feet. It was totally empty, too. Crossing that room took you to a concrete wall that had a metal door and a one way glass the full length of the upper half of the wall. This is from where the guards observed you 24 hours a day and thus the name, "the Fishbowl".

The wall behind me was concrete and had a door at each end. Both doors led into a huge padded cell.

I looked through a slit in one of the doors and saw a skinny naked body of a man curled up in the corner of the padded cell. Everyday a guard and a nurse came to the slit in the door and stood and watched this body until the nurse would finally say, "He's alive, I saw him move." And then they would push his food through the slot and leave. I never saw anything else come out nor did anyone ever go in. They just observed through the slit in the door until they could see him breathing.

I saw no one in the other padded cell.

They threw me a thin blanket and a roll of toilet paper and at meal times they brought a tray and slid a box that had a sandwich and Kool-Aid into the padded cell.

There was nothing else in this long narrow room of mine, no table, no chair, no sink, and no toilet, just me. They popped the lock on the empty padded cell when I had to go to the bathroom and the rest of the time, for a better part of a week, I sat there on the floor doing nothing. When I wasn't sitting I was trying to sleep under the thin blanket using the roll of toilet paper for my pillow. No shower, no brushing teeth, no washing face, no one to talk with, no TV, no radio, no window, no clock, no dimming of the bright lights, *no nothing*.

This was a perfect place to go nuts from this type of treatment because you were conveniently sitting next to an empty padded cell.

I figured the time to be a week by the occurrences of meals. I would roll up a small wad of toilet paper every time I thought a day had passed. As those wads grew in number I realized where my life was heading. Prison began to look good from where I was right now. I thought of that skinny naked body, who I saw curled up in the corner of that padded cell, and I was amazed that, in this day and age, it was still possible for one human being to be lost and never heard from again. I imagined that one day a body could just be tossed out with the garbage. As I pressed my face to the peep hole in the door to the padded cell, I came face to face with being so totally lost that no one would know what corner of your life you were curled up in.

Life becomes more real after being this close to the death of it.

Even this side of society called "good" can close their eyes to humanity and find evil. Our institutions in the criminal justice system take crime to heights that street criminals have never thought to go. After all, these institutions are run by *professionals* when it comes to crime. Your treatment in prison will always be a heavier crime against your personal 'humanity' than the crime you committed on the street. Incarceration is a glaring, flagrant example of the truth that *life is not fair.*

I was being watched and probably even filmed while I was in the "fishbowl", and so I built myself a little community in my mind. I tried to structure my sleeping hours and when I was awake, during what I thought to be day time hours, I folded my one thin blanket and laid it neatly against the wall and placed the toilet paper pillow on top. I walked around my 6x18 foot area as I tried to remember scripture, and I recited poetry and I carried on conversations with myself.

I made a big show of exercising regularly by doing jumping jacks, which were never a part of any exercise program of mine, but this was "show and tell" and jumping jacks were big movements. I wanted my actions to tell anyone who was watching, "I'm Ok...let me out of here...don't turn me into a vegetable...I'm Ok...see?"

I had nine wads of toilet paper in my corner near the wall but the doctor said I was in there 6 days. My mind was disoriented. I didn't care about anything but convincing the doctor that I wasn't going to kill everyone in the state of Georgia starting with the guards and ending with myself.

I smiled at the doctor who didn't smile back, "I was just spouting off. I just wanted out because I couldn't accept responsibility. I was wrong for the crimes I committed and I can face up to the punishment now."

It was going to be his decision as to whether I go back to a cell block or to the fishbowl or to the next step, the padded cell. I knew I was groveling by what I was saying. I thought how utterly insane of me to try so hard to appear to be sane in all this insanity. In the crime I committed that caused me to be arrested, I felt I was in the right, but now I'm admitting how wrong I was because a lie is all anyone wants to hear.

If they knew I thought I was punished for something I didn't do, it would be too hard for me to convince them that I could handle the injustice. Since the doctor only comes by once a week I groveled and I took a stance against this terrible person called 'me' and I vowed to look down on the vile person that I was.

It made them happy.

That's what I wanted to do…make them happy.

The relief was indescribable when he called the guard and said he was filing the papers for me to go back to 'B-Pod.'

That must have meant I was Ok to them, which scared me, because that just proved I was insane. I still couldn't watch people through the window or people on TV. I just couldn't do that. But I never wanted to take another nose dive and end up back in the "fishbowl" either.

I actually found the 7th floor NW, B-Pod, cell 408…home sweet home.

As soon as the locks popped for our turn in the day room I grabbed my bible and went looking for Herb. We sat across the room from the TV as usual and I started in, "Herb, what do they mean about being anointed? Can I get anointed? Who has to anoint you? How is it done? My prayers aren't working because I'm not anointed. I'll bet you anything, that's what it is."

It appeared as though Herb was pleased and frustrated at the same time. His thinking might have been that I was getting the message but I'm not hearing it right. Herb told me to turn to Luke 4:1 "Read what that says."

I did.

"Now read Luke 4:14.

I did.

"You see Duke, Jesus was *full* of the Holy Spirit when he returned from Jordan and he was led by the spirit into the desert and he fasted for forty days. At the end of forty days Jesus was tempted by the devil. But notice what it says in Luke 4:14, it says Jesus returned to Galilee *in the power* of the Spirit. And you see further down where He reads from Isaiah, *the Spirit of the Lord is on me, because He has anointed me.*"

I nodded excitedly, "Ok, ok, that's cool…so what do I have to do to be anointed?"

"Stay in the Spirit and hide God's word in your heart. One day you will feel the Spirit take you over and you will feel His power in your life."

"Yeah, alright, but how about now…you know, I mean, can you anoint me? You know a lot of this stuff or does it have to be a real preacher? Can that last preacher man anoint me?"

Herb was shaking his head as soon as I started but I rushed through it before he told me, "There isn't anything you can do to acquire it, you just stay with your walk, stay in the Spirit and it will be something that happens to you. Isaiah said, the Spirit of the Lord *is on me*, because he has anointed me."

That sounded too hocus pocus to me and I didn't want to have to wait for the Lord to see that I earned this anointing. I didn't think this was going to work for me. Anyway the people who say they're anointed speak funny. They say things I can't understand and tell me they are speaking "in tongues". I was told that since God was a spirit, the spirit in you has got to move you to speak "in tongues".

I couldn't do that and so I felt very un-spiritual and ungodly.

But I also read that in order to do any good, this "gift", of speaking in tongues, needs someone to interpret so that everyone listening would understand what is being said. I can't help but believe God knows any language we choose to speak and I doubt that praying is a matter of what type of "speaking" is being done.

While searching for something "useable" to my life in the study of God, I began to acquire a feeling I couldn't explain. I couldn't describe the feeling I had any more accurately, than to repeat the words Napoleon said about how he once felt. He said, "I feel myself driven to an end that I do not know." And that is what I felt while searching for the secrets, hidden in plain sight, within God's Word. All the answers for which I searched stared at me from the pages of my bible but I couldn't see them. The only peace I felt in prison came from the knowledge that I would eventually find the answers I needed if I sought them earnestly.

The bible said "knock and a door would be opened unto you…seek and ye shall find." The word "earnestly" seems to pop up in my head when I think these things. But was I searching for answers earnestly, or did I only search for those answers that I thought would serve my own purpose?

Ephesians 1:18 said to pray that the "Eyes of your understanding be enlightened so that you may know what is the hope of His calling"…the purpose He has for my life. It is to that end I feel driven.

Napoleon said, "*I feel myself driven to an end I do not know. As soon as I have reached it, as soon as I shall become unnecessary, an atom will suffice to shatter me. Until then, not all the forces of mankind can do anything against me!*"

Maybe I will face a Waterloo too some day but for now, my battle is neither with "mankind" nor with flesh and blood. A war is taking place in the heavenly realm and the principalities are battling for my soul. One day my body will be unnecessary, but before I am shattered, the eyes of my understanding will be enlightened and I will know the hope of God's calling for my life.

32

Each day was so much the same as the day before.

We did nothing but lie on our racks and wait for time to pass. To say you're doing "easy" time in county means you sleep a lot. I wasn't doing my time "easy". My brain was too active to sleep.

"Ray, you going to church meeting tonight?"

There was no answer.

I pressed on, "I came across something here that says…here; I'll read it." I turned to John 14:14 and read out loud, "You may ask for anything in my name and I will do it." As I pondered those words I sat up and then got out of bed. I put down my bible and used the urinal. When I was finished I sat back down on the edge of my bunk before saying, "I always pray in the name of Jesus, why is it not…"

Ray rolled towards the wall and in a serious but low voice said, "Shut up Duke, I'm sleeping."

I had one person in the world to talk with and he is doing his time "easy". I don't know how he does it. I couldn't understand why he wasn't trying to find out how to use God to get him out. I shrugged it off and went into my own head and pondered this thought and vowed to be sure that I always said "In the name of Jesus" whenever I prayed.

In the weeks that followed I prayed and I prayed and I prayed and I always prayed by beginning with, "In the name of Jesus." When I said grace before meals I always started by saying "In the name of Jesus" and when I led prayer in bible study I'd say it again, and if I wanted to mix it up a little, to show the others I was pretty good at praying, I would say it at the beginning and at the end. I was covering myself on both sides.

I didn't see anything happening though, I didn't feel anything happening, and to tell you the truth I didn't believe anything was happening. I prayed to get out of jail, but I prayed for lesser things too, just to see if it would happen and to test my prayers. I prayed that my daughter would write me a letter and that my son would visit me. I used "In the name of Jesus" but it wasn't happening as I thought it would. It wasn't happening at all.

I imagined Herb was losing his patience with me. I'm surprised he continued to try and teach me but he did the best he could, and his efforts may have been working, but it was slow in coming. Then, on top of everything else, and with all the time I had on my hands, I couldn't figure why I had no patience. The only thing I could figure was that I was so anxious to get out; time flew by me while I was in my search of the right formula. I knew there must be something that would do the trick. Prison was not the place for me.

I wanted to be free.

It had been months ago that I first heard about "anointing" and it's been several weeks since I discovered I was supposed to pray in the name of Jesus.

I was a bit confused on all this stuff.

I found others who were searching the Word for answers and I sensed that many of them were struggling just like me with the understanding of it.

This morning my name was called to go to court and I had some wonderful hopes that maybe someone got me an attorney or someone has been pleading my case. But more often than not, when I was called to go to court unexpectedly it usually meant there was another charge popping up somewhere, with new information from another "witness", or a fresh set of fingerprints that were found somewhere to match mine.

I didn't get excited anymore about riding over to the court house.

A few of us were pulled from each pod and put into a holding cell until there were over sixty of us in a cell designed for half that many at the most.

A short thin Cuban was talking about his family in Cuba and how he was here in the states so that he could visit his grandson. He talked about his grandson's Christening and how much he enjoyed seeing him. He talked about his life in Cuba and that if he got out of the mess that he was in, he was going to talk his daughter into coming back to Cuba with him. He wasn't talking to anyone in particular; he took turns pointing his face in the direction of different men in the cell as different thoughts came to him. He said, "My grandson will know about Christ...he won't end up like me..." he paused and then said, "or his father."

He was a small man and said that he killed his son in law in self-defense. His son-in-law had a history of beating the Cuban man's daughter but one night the son-in-law was so drunk he was going after his grandson with a butcher knife. The little Cuban man went in the other room, got a gun, came back and shot his son-in-law in the head.

He said, "I could got away but because of all the yelling, the cops were all ready on the way, before I even shot him."

"When that one cop came through the door I got scared and shot at him." He said, "I yelled out and said I just want to go home to Cuba, and take my grandson and daughter with me."

We all listened quietly to his story. The little Cuban man said, "Now...look at me. I should a killed the cops, too."

Something prompted me to say, "No, I don't think so. I think it's going to be all right...but killing a cop, no...that wouldn't be good."

"What?" He shouted and moved over and stood in front of where I was sitting. "I just killed Alfredo and if I killed the cops too, I would be in Cuba right now."

"No you wouldn't...you'd be dead." I said.

In an instant he had turned his anger on me, "Who the hell are you?"

I looked around and saw everyone staring at me and suddenly I realized these were all strangers. They're not the guys in my section who know each other, and have come to know when to say something, or when to keep their mouth shut. Obviously, the Cuban just needed to spout off and wasn't looking for anyone else to enter into his world. That's the way it is you know. Sometimes, an angry person is just mouthing off in hopes that someone else will say something, anything, it doesn't matter what. The person mouthing off is just brewing for a fight.

It looked as though everyone was expecting me to answer this little guy's challenge. I didn't want to go back to the hole. I already spent six days in the "fishbowl" and I didn't want to go back.

"Why don't you stand up or shut your mouth," he said.

My silence was misread and it spurred his courage and so he continued, "Come on stand up or do you want it right where you sit."

I was clearly going to have to do something; everyone was watching to see if I was going to stand up, speak up or fight. Except for this Cuban and me, everyone else was black and for me to back down now would be a bad thing for me to do. I didn't want to hurt this skinny little old man but what else was I supposed to do.

This was not the place to be nice and this guy just killed somebody and was riding high on some power trip, so I stood up. But instead of hitting him, I said, "OK man, have it your way but after I dump your head in that toilet, how is your grandson going to learn about Jesus?"

He stood and looked at me for a very long moment. I didn't know what he was planning to do and I didn't know who else here was on his side, so I cautiously waited for him to make his move.

He finally made it.

My eyes widened when he reached his hand into his jumpsuit. I looked at all the rough and scarred faces around the room and tried to determine if any of these characters would be backing him up. They were a hard, mean looking bunch and it was obvious that they were anxious to see some action.

When he pulled his hand out of his jumpsuit I saw a small black object in his hand and a cold chill grabbed me and I stiffened. I brought my hands up as I took a quick breath in and held it. He looked at me defiantly and took one step forward and said, "So, what do you know about Jesus?" I had to pry myself away from his dark sunken eyes to glimpse at what he had in his hand. I did a double take when I saw the weapon he pulled out. It wasn't a pipe, razor, or a knife, he was holding the perfect weapon; a small black bible.

I looked over at someone I knew from B-Pod and he exhaled and then took in a quick short breath and held that one as several of these men closed in around us. Someone standing just two feet away took a step closer and he brought out a bible too. Another prisoner put his foot up on the bench and bent over and pulled a small bible out of his sock.

Everyone else moved in closer and someone repeated the Cuban's question, "So what do you know about Jesus?"

I was so shocked, so profoundly shocked that I wanted to laugh. I didn't want to laugh at them, I just felt relief and joy in realizing I was not alone. We all want to know more about Jesus but we hide that fact until someone says it's alright, until someone takes a stand for Jesus. We all think we'll be thought of as weak if we rely on the strength Christ wants us to use, His strength.

We all have the same questions about God, but rather than ask anyone, we hide behind the guise of being too tough to care and we wait for someone else to risk looking weak. But once it's out of the bag, and we see it's alright to go there, we pull out our hidden thoughts and feel safe to expose them as we go after what we so desperately need to know.

I remembered Herb telling me that God's work could be done right here, and now I saw how right he was. Everyone here was hungry; there was a serious thirst in all of us to know God. I said, "I know He doesn't want us wasting our lives in here and I believe he's going to get us out."

"What does scripture say?" A voice from the middle of the crowd asked.

Someone else answered, "Proverbs 17:26 says it is not good to punish an innocent man and I didn't do what they said I did."

The guy next to me waved it off, "Aw, don't you worry none; look here, Romans says that there is no condemnation for those who are in Christ Jesus."

One by one, these men revealed some scripture on which they had been leaning. More than two thirds of us were going to court armed with a bible hidden on us somewhere. I hoped the rest at least had some 'Word' hidden in their heart.

Scripture after scripture was being shared as more inmates joined in and pulled out bibles that were hidden in some secret place. What followed was an impromptu bible study with arguments and heated debates; because with *us*, the "Word" was more than read, it was argued over and fought over, and what we finally agreed upon, was prayed over. We wanted to be sure that we were getting it straight because we relied heavily on being able to find some scripture that we could apply to our situation to help us, not only our cause or desire of being released, but most of us really discovered we wanted God's Word to help us change our lives.

When it was time to put us on the bus a guard unlocked the door and swung it open and yelled, "Listen up for your name…Anderson, Dominique, Swayze…"

Ignoring the guard, one of the prisoners asked, "Who wants to pray?"

The guard repeated louder, "I said listen up for your name…answer up and step out…Anderson, Dominique…"

We all began shifting around so that we could join hands.

The guard tried again but we continued moving around and directing each other until we all had a hold of a hand and some big fellow who hadn't said a thing up until now said, "Dear Father God, in the name of Jesus…" and we had begun to pray. By this time the guard was cussing and yelling threats at us and demanding that we stop and listen and move out into the hall when we heard our name. But we ignored him and stood with heads bowed as our brother went on praying as though we were in a quiet peaceful sanctuary.

An officer in plain clothes tapped the guard on the arm and gestured by shaking his head and lifting his finger to his lips and the guard was silenced and while we all prayed together, I was having a private prayer of my own, "Dear Lord please do not let me forget this day or my brothers here who shared this moment with me."

Sixty of us prisoners, every last one of us, held hands and we finished our prayer as the guards stood by and waited.

I remembered what Herb said about plenty of work to do for the Lord right here.

A huge bell rang in my heart for me that day. It woke me to the realization that people want to talk about Jesus, they just want to know it's "alright" first.

So like little boys we stand around and wait for some other little boy to say it's alright for us to be a man.

It was a long time before I knew that it wasn't anyone else's call to determine who or what I was. I used to look to other men and women to see me as the man I never knew myself to be. I thought that if they could see me as the man I had hoped to be, than sooner or later, maybe I'd see me there too.

All of us in here were in the same boat to some degree or the other. We've looked deep into drugs, alcohol, violence, and relationships, and all those other things outside ourselves, to measure who we were and why.

The mirrors I used in order to see myself were shattered early on in life. And, throughout my life I've been searching in other persons, places and things to find a mirror that reflected back to me the image I hoped I would see.

Little did I know then, what I am starting to find out now; God has the perfect mirror for me; and His name is Jesus.

33

The preacher tonight seemed to hit another nail right on the head for me.

I would start my prayer by saying, "In the name of Jesus" because I was told to say it, or else our prayer wouldn't be answered.

But the preacher tonight told us that our prayers were not being answered because we were not praying in the name of Jesus. I objected to this charge but he persisted in claiming that we were not praying in the name of Jesus because we didn't *know* the name of Jesus.

That was disturbing.

At this time in my life I was praying a lot. I was praying that I wouldn't have to spend the rest of my life in prison but now I'm told that I didn't even know the name I was supposed to use when I prayed.

No wonder my prayers weren't working for me.

I asked everybody I could about this dilemma about the correct name of Jesus to use but no one could tell me anything that helped. The pastor who preached this message confused me more when he tried to answer the questions I had for him. I got the impression that he knew the name because he was anointed, gifted, or blessed in some special way. He knew a lot about the bible, and so I believed everything he said. I wished so hard that I could be like these people who could remember all those pretty King James Version scriptures and spout them off in response to some question a person had.

That preacher, and a lot of other folks, said they could speak in tongues because they have received that gift. It was a process of praying in the spirit, and since God was a spirit, that was they way one talked to God, in the spirit.

The further I got into the Word with people who had been walking this walk longer than I, the more confused I became. I started to think I've been discarded and I was not wanted by God.

My prayers didn't work, I couldn't speak in tongues, and I didn't even know the name Jesus wants me to call Him.

Months of discouragement followed as well as frustration and anger. I turned hostile and bitter as I attacked God's Word and challenged all these super righteous thoughts. It looked like everyone else was gifted and everyone else knew secrets I didn't deserve to be in on. But I had no place else to go and so I plugged away and tried to learn more of God in hopes that it wasn't too late for me.

I discovered that there were several names for God and for Jesus, and even different names for the Holy Ghost.

The biblical concept of naming was rooted in the ancient world's understanding that a name expressed essence, and to know the name of a person was to know that person's total character and nature. The name given God was different with each different function he performed and such names for God as Elohim, Jehovah, El-Shaddai, Yahweh-Jireh, Yahweh-Nissi, Adonai denote what He would do for you.

The handling of God's name had its rules. When the name Yahweh is used to denote God's name, it was spelled with only the four consonants YHWH. This was God's name in Hebrew known by the technical term "Tetragrammaton". There are four consonants which make up the divine name and they are found more than 6000 times in the Old Testament. Since Hebrew language did not include vowels, only the consonants were used; thus readers supplied the vowels as they read.

Reverence for the divine name led to the practice of avoiding the use of it, lest one run afoul of the commandments. The commandment in Exodus 20:7 "thou shall not take the name of the Lord thy God in vain," gave rise to the thought that the divine name was too holy to pronounce at all.

I read where a supposed scholar determined the name of God should be Elohim or Adonai, which somehow makes the Holy Spirit's name Qodesh Ruach and the name of Christ Jesus to be Yahshua Mashiach. This scholar goes on to ask, "Shouldn't we make the effort to address Him by that name?"

I corresponded with this man in order to find out if that in fact is what I should do.

Somehow, because I was incarcerated, we got into an argument about my right to ask such questions from him, and that surprised me. If I received anything at all from corresponding with this so-called "authority" on God's Word, it was how human and frail we all are, even those of us who appear the strongest.

I thought that surely this was my out. This man could have told me the name to use when I pray and he wouldn't. Was this part of my punishment? I actually found where I could go for answers, and in a strange turn of events, someone refused to let me have them.

Herb saw that I was beyond being disappointed and that I was in a deep state of depression. He came over and sat at the table with me. I was frustrated that I would not be trusted with these Godly secrets that everyone knows.

Herb said, "How's it going?"

"It's not. Remember that preacher we had in here a while back; why did he have to say all that?"

"That skinny guy from Roswell?"

"No…a while back. The guy who said we don't pray in the name of Jesus because we don't know the name of Jesus, and then he wouldn't tell me what it was."

Herb nodded, smiled and I think I noticed a slight shake of his head as if he couldn't believe I was still worried about something someone said so long ago.

"I don't believe him, you know. But I can't find the scripture to tell me why, nor can I find the understanding to tell me why not…I don't even know what I'm looking for."

"You mean the name of Jesus, the name to use when you pray?"

I slowly bobbed my head up and down, "I just don't get it. I think he's wrong, you know…that preacher guy. How could they let a preacher like him in here if he's going to get our heads all screwed up?"

Herb smiled as though he were admitting to a mischievous secret, "You're right, he's wrong."

"What? You know? I mean, he is? Then why haven't you said anything, why didn't you set him straight?"

"That's not my doings. I don't set people straight. I listen to what they have to say and then I check it out for myself."

"Then how do you know whether they're right or wrong?"

"I check it against scripture."

"You mean preachers would come in here and tell us things that are not right with scripture?"

"Hey man…preachers are just people. They interpret scripture the best they can and not everyone sees it the same."

"How can that be? Why do you even listen to them then?"

"Same reason I eat chicken."

"Eat chicken?"

"That's right. You eat chicken, don't you?"

I couldn't answer because I couldn't figure where he was going with it.

Herb repeated himself, "I said; you do eat chicken, don't you?"

"Of course I do."

"Do you eat the bones?"

"No."

"Me neither. I eat the meat and throw away the bones. I know there's going to be bones in chicken but that doesn't stop me from eating the meat."

I smiled and made a mental note to remember that example.

Herb said, "Now get me John 14:14 and read it."

"Ok", I read, *"You may ask me anything in my name and I will do it."*

"Turn to John 17:11 and read me that."

I read, *"Holy Father, protect them by the power of your name—the name you gave me—so that they may be one as we are one."*

Herb said, "You see, it was the Father who gave Jesus a name. He said 'protect them by the power of your name…the name *you* gave me.' And Duke, when you ask everyone else, of course you're going to get confused. People through the ages called Christ many things, and the things they called Him became the names *they* gave Him. But in John 17:11 it says that the Holy Father gave Christ a name. Do you know what it was?"

"You know I don't." I was getting excited to think Herb was going to tell me and at the same time I was irritated because he wouldn't just come out and tell me, "Well, come on Herb, why you messing with me? Just tell me, what was it?"

I saw Herb give me that look when he had enough of me. He had a way he wanted to teach and I embarrassed him when I criticized his ways. I could see he was about ready to shut me off. He scowled and I sensed he was ready to get up and leave. My impatience was rude and it set him off again. If he walks away now it could be weeks before he talks to me and then I might never find what I need to know.

I took a deep breath and held it and said something I rarely told anyone before, "I'm sorry." This seemed to stop him from leaving but I saw it wasn't enough and so I added, "Don't stop now...I'll shut up...I promise."

The devil can't curse what God has blessed and so he helps us act in such a way that we pull ourselves out of the blessed place, and we end up cursing ourselves. Herb was close to telling me what I've been looking for all these months. It was something I thought would help me get out of here. I got impatient and blew it. Our war is not against flesh and blood, I humbled myself, "Herb, please." I paused, "Look man, I'm sorry."

I didn't consciously realize how close Herb was to getting up to leave until then. I saw the lines on his forehead flatten and he relaxed his shoulders. Then he turned back towards me and in his low strong voice he said, "Ok, turn to Matthew."

I did.

Herb said, "Read Matthew 1:21".

I read, *"She (Mary) will give birth to a son and you are to give him the name Jesus."* I stopped and looked at Herb. "Well that says it right there...so what is all this stuff about me not praying in the name of Jesus because I *don't know the name of Jesus?"*

Herb shrugged, "Look at verse 23."

*"Behold a virgin shall be with child, and shall bring forth a son, and they shall call his name Emmanuel...*hey, wait a minute. Now this says his name is Emmanuel."

"Don't let that throw you."

"Well, I'll be…" My anger was about to show again and I had to make an effort to curb it, "which one is it, Herb?"

In that moment that was split in time before Herb responded, it seemed as though I had all the time in the world to think back on all the occasions I argued with God. I thought of all the times I got mad at God because I couldn't understand the bible. I couldn't help but think that if I talked the way they did in this bible no one could understand me either. It seemed obvious that people would get mad and not want to talk with me anymore, but I couldn't be that way. I needed to understand this; I was drawn to the bible as if it were my only chance to get out. I had to keep coming back to it. I had to understand it.

Herb said, "Read it closer."

"I don't have to read it closer. See, it says in the 21st verse that the name is Jesus and in the 23rd verse it's Emmanuel." I was right on this one, I found a flaw in the bible and I was going to nail Herb to the wall on this one. "How clear does it have to be?

There were times Herb would just get up and walk away when I got into my self righteous mode but this time Herb showed patience, "Here's a perfect example of what happens when you either read out of context or you don't know enough scripture to know what it is you're reading."

"I'm not reading it out of context. I read the whole verse, both of them."

"You read the 21st and the 23rd but what about the 22nd?"

My answer was too quick and there was an edge to my tone, "That doesn't say anything about his name."

Herb shot me a look and shook his head in disbelief.

"Whaaa…aat?" The stupid look on my face must have coaxed him to stay, "It doesn't, does it?"

The bench and table, where we sat, was made of smooth stainless steel and bolted to the floor. Herb leaned forward on his forearms and drummed his fingers on the top of the metal table as he looked away. He was irritated but he was trying to have patience with me. It was clear by his behavior that I was wrong again. I really wasn't sure what it was I said that was so bad, but just the same, I immediately dispelled the thought that I found a flaw in God's Word and quickly acknowledged the flaw was in me.

I thought I knew what he was thinking. How could he possibly teach me a thing about Christ when I am so ignorant when it comes to scripture?

He stopped drumming and turned back to me. His effort to put up with my ignorance was evident that he wanted to get this message through to me as earnestly as I wanted to receive it.

He went on with his explanation, "The 22nd verse tells us that verse 23 is making reference to the old testament prophet, Isaiah, and is stating the prophecy which was given in Isaiah 7:14."

"But his name…it says…"

"Can you tell me where Jesus was ever called Emmanuel?"

"No, but…"

Herb tried to suppress his irritability but still, his voice grew louder, his tone sharper and his pace got quicker as he explained, "That's right, He wasn't. He is called Jesus because that is His name. He was given this name because He will save His people from their sins. Christ is His title; Jesus is His name. When interpreted, Emmanuel means God with us and He can't be Emmanuel, *God with us*, unless He is virgin born. And notice, unless He is Emmanuel, He cannot be Jesus the Savior. The reason they call Him Jesus, Savior, is because He is God with us." He paused and then added softly, "His name is Jesus."

That stayed with me as he was telling it to me, but as soon as Herb was finished, I lost it all, every bit of it. I just wasn't able to remember all that scripture. Herb must be right about all this though, and so I was satisfied and I decided to stick with the name, Jesus. But I was still confused about what people tell us, "But why then, I just can't understand why that preacher says we don't know his name."

"What did I say earlier? Keep the meat and throw away the bones. If you stay in the Word you will know which is which."

"Well, if I'm praying with the correct name why does it appear to me that my prayers aren't being heard?"

Herb said, "Now we're getting somewhere. You might be heading in the right direction now. It's possible you don't know what the word "name" means," and then he put me back in pursuit of more scripture, "Read John 10:25-26".

I read, *"The miracles I do in my Father's name speak for me, but you do not believe because you are not my sheep."*

I looked up at Herb and said, "I don't get it."

"Do you really think that you are praying in the name of Jesus just because you say the words, *'in the name of Jesus'* when you pray? Those are just words and that isn't what it means to pray in the name of Jesus."

The PA system made the announcement, "Lockdown".

It was time to get back to my cell.

It was just as well, I think I was trying Herb's patience again. He gets irritable when I can't understand what he's talking about. I didn't want to get him mad at me now that I was getting somewhere with this.

I was not sure where, but if I didn't get Herb frustrated, I might find out.

34

I sat down on my bunk. It looked like Ray was already asleep. We get a lot of sleep doing county time. Sleep has become a habit that we can fall right into as quickly as closing our eyes. I wasn't sleepy one bit and so I didn't think I'd be sleeping for a long while yet.

But the moment my head hit my blanket I was out.

When my eyes opened I felt rested and wide awake. I don't know how long I slept but it looked to be coming up on lunch time. I laid there and tried to remember everything Herb was trying to get me to see earlier.

Without any prompting, a thought popped into my head.

I don't know why.

I let it in.

A vision of a girl who used to be very pretty came to me. Too much speed took the meat from her bones. The dope sunk her eyes deep into her head and put dark circles under them. She always looked like someone just gave her two black eyes.

I knew this girl.

Not only did I know her when she was down and out, I knew her the night I put my gun into her mouth and stripped her of her jewelry. It was to pay a debt she owed for drugs and I was just doing my job. I knew her when she was put in jail, because she was with her boyfriend when he held up a convenience store.

And more vivid than anything, I knew her two years later when I ran into a cleaned up and prosperous version of her. She had straightened out and I was actually embarrassed to see her this time. This was when we had one last talk and she told me she forgave me a long time ago.

That was just a chance meeting, and as she left me that day she put something in my hand, rose up on her toes and kissed me on the cheek and without another word, turned and walked away. I haven't seen her since.

What she gave me was a bible tract, which I crumpled up and threw away, but the words she wrote across it stayed with me to this day, "God loves you and so do I."

It looks like I stepped into her own brand of ministry, and I could only imagine how she felt, slipping a piece of forgiveness into the hand that once jammed a .44 Bulldog revolver in her mouth and cocked the hammer back.

I knew this girl.

We had a history like very few others.

I lay still while I struggled to remember more.

There was something else to remember but I couldn't think of what it was. There was some reason this incident came to me and I was trying to understand what that reason was.

And then, like a flashbulb exploding in my face, I suddenly caught on.

I jumped up and said out loud, "That's what it is…. I can't remember her name…I don't *know her name*…but *I know her*."

"Great, just great" Ray pulled his blanket up over his head, "now shut up and let me sleep."

I wrote down what I could remember, so I wouldn't forget to bring it up to Herb and see what he thought it all meant.

That night when we were let out of the cell, Herb and I talked. I told him about the incident that happened years ago and how vividly it came back to me this afternoon. I told him why I thought I was thinking of it now, and asked his take on it.

Herb agreed with me, "In biblical times the knowing of a name implied a *relationship* between parties in which power to do harm or good was in force. The important part is that you had a relationship with that girl in a way that you knew something about her. The actual letters and sounds those letters make when you speak her name is not as important as the relationship you had of knowing her."

I was starting to understand where Herb was leading me. He took me to John 16:26-27. Jesus was talking to his disciples He said, "In that day you will ask in my name. I am not saying that I will ask the Father on your behalf. No, the Father himself loves you *because you have loved me* and *believe I came from God.*"

Accepting the statement Jesus said, "*You have loved me and believe*" is the relationship one is referring to when they say "In the name of Jesus."

Herb had the answer for which I was looking but he wanted me to find it for myself. So then I said, "When I ask "in the name of Jesus" I am not asking Jesus to go to the Father and plead my case. I am saying that the name on that check I'm using, that is the name of Jesus and I am authorized to use that check the same as Jesus would use it."

Herb nodded, "Galatians 4:7, '*Wherefore thou art no more a servant, but a son; and if a son, than an heir of God through Christ*' then we have the same rights as He does".

That's *relationship*…our relationship, and the reason I can truly say I come to God *in the name of Jesus.*

I was beginning to see that when I pray, "in the name of Jesus", I am saying, "Lord, Jesus is your son and because of the *relationship* I have with him, I am yours too." I said, "Herb…if I won't accept Him in my life except under my own conditions, then I don't have the relationship I say I have."

Herb smiled

35

Sometimes when we mention a famous name, in association with ourselves, we want people to think we know that person more than we really do.

That does happen some times. We do that because we want that person, with whom we're talking, to think we have a relationship with that famous person. A relationship that really doesn't exist the way we say it does. We think we are thought of differently because of it, and sometimes we benefit from having other people think we have an "in" with that important person.

To say the words, "In the name of Jesus", meant nothing at all. They were just empty words, and mean nothing, unless there truly is a relationship that exists between you and Jesus.

It isn't the "name" you're saying it's "what" you have with Jesus by saying "in the name of Jesus". What you are saying is that you "know" Jesus and that you have a relationship with him, so whether the letters spell the words *Yahshua Mashiach; Iesous Christos;* or *Kurios Iesous Christos*, or simply *Jesus*, it doesn't matter to God. What God really wants us to be truthful about is; do we really "know" Jesus, or are we just name-dropping? Do we experience Jesus, and do we really have a relationship with him, or do we just say we do?

But God knows our hearts and He knows what relationship exists between us.

One day I gave in.

There isn't any other way to describe the change that took place in me other than to say that *I came to myself.* I saw the insincerity in what I was telling God and I studied His word purely for my own self serving purpose. I saw the futility in what I was trying do.

For months now, I have been trying to pray and say that I would accept Christ, even if it meant I had to live the rest of my life in prison. I haven't been able to say the words. I got as far as saying, "Lord…it's Ok, I will stay…I will." I would pause for quite awhile and then burst out with, "God, I promise I will work for you when I get out, but please don't make me stay here, let me out. I will be too old to do anything for you in twenty years."

This was not the relationship God had for me at all.

And so, one day I finally let the words out. I finally realized that I wanted the relationship more than I wanted anything else. And so, I said, "Lord, thank you for loving me. Forgive me for all I've done wrong. Come into my life and help me become the person you created me to be. Come into my life right here, right now, I need your help. I remove all conditions by which I ask you to come into my life. If I am to stay in prison, if I am to get out, it doesn't matter as long as I can spend my life with you."

Before that prayer was over, Jesus Christ truly entered my heart. I didn't wish for His help to get out of prison, or His help for an easier life, I just wanted Him.

I didn't accept Him because I hoped my conditions would get better. I plainly said that I would rather have Christ in my life and stay behind bars than to walk out of prison without Him.

Wherever He was is where I wanted to be.

I was free…I was behind bars but I was finally free. It was only after I said, "OK Lord, whatever you want me to do…I am yours" that I truly had a relationship with Jesus.

I now knew what it felt like to accept the issue of death and be totally at peace with it. The feeling came over me that if I were to die that very minute it was perfectly alright with me. I would be happy because I know I would be with God. But what was more amazing was that not only did I lose my fear of dying I also lost my fear of living.

When I was afraid of life and everything in it, I didn't cower down and tremble in the corner. Very few of us living a scared existence do that. Instead, we strut about and boast and bully and are quick to anger. Being scared is not what most people would recognize as being behavior like that, but that is what it is. It is being greedy, unfair, unkind, and mean, because that's the behavior that stems from being afraid.

We are afraid we're not going to get all we think we have the right to have or else we become afraid that we'll lose what we have.

We get lost in drugs, alcohol, and illicit affairs as a way of hiding from what scares us. There's not a person alive who hasn't had a fear that pushed them into some poor choice at one time or another.

Since the day I accepted Jesus into my life Herb let me help him with the bible studies and he didn't get frustrated with me anymore. I helped counsel the younger men who had a difficult time adjusting to life in jail and I made friends with people I didn't think I would get along with. I felt as though I now had a home and it wasn't the Dekalb County Detention Center, the home was having Jesus in my heart.

I no longer prayed that I would get out.

I prayed instead, that I could serve God and help people find strength through Christ as I did. He answered my prayer by helping me drop the barrier I constructed to keep Jesus away. When He answered my prayer and gave me peace I was perfectly happy behind bars helping others and learning about Christ from Herb.

Christ said to His disciples, "If any man will come after me, let him deny himself, and take up his cross daily; and follow me. For whosoever shall save his life shall lose it: but whosoever shall lose his life for my sake, the same shall save it."

A few months after I accepted my relationship with Jesus, I was surprised with an unexpected announcement. It was in the middle of our morning time out of the cell, and I was talking with Herb about our next prayer meeting, when out of the blue, for no reason I could possibly imagine, a loud voice yelled over the PA system, "Duke Tirschel…bag and baggage."

I was talking to Herb and didn't even think to respond. I heard the announcement but the words it was saying didn't register with me. They repeated it, "Duke Tirschel I said, NOW, *bag and baggage.*"

Some of the other inmates came running over to me and said, "What's wrong with you man, can't you hear? They're calling for you…*bag and baggage*…you're outta here."

"They must have made a mistake. I don't have any action going on...nothing's pending on me except two counts of armed robbery."

I guarded my curiosity carefully. I didn't want to hope for something that would come crashing down on me once the mistake was discovered. I walked across the day room and pressed the buzzer, "This is Duke. Did you call my name?"

The voice coming through the box said, "Are you Tirschel?"

"Yes"

"Then get your stuff and bring it to the door."

"But what..."

The guard yelled back, "You want to argue? You have two minutes to get your gear or I'll make it so you can stay."

I walked over to where Herb was sitting and said, "Well, I guess I have to leave. We were just getting things together. I really don't want to go." I had the strangest feeling that they should have given me some notice, but then, the thought *I'm getting out* was screaming in my chest. It was cold ticklish feeling that felt great when I took a deep breath. The absolute surprise and disbelief made me fumble through my 'stuff' as I gave my extra pillow to the first person who asked, my pads of paper to Mark, my stamps to Ray. I had an extra blanket that I gave to Ray too, along with a razor blade I had hid. I used it for cutting strips of sheets that I braided and used to make my jump rope. I gave the balance of my "store" to Herb. It included some Hot Fries, 3 bags of chips, and two cups of heat and eat soup, a moon pie, and a couple packages of Oreo's. It was quite a haul for Herb.

The PA sounded again, "Duke Tirschel...bag and baggage...last call."

I walked over to Herb and said, "Goodbye Herb. Well, I guess I got to go."

Herb was tinkering around with nothing too important but he kept his focus on the trivial task at hand. He balled up his fist and with his thumb he jerked his hand towards the door over his shoulder and in a tough and gruff voice said, "Go on, get out of here," and then, without looking up he added, "and don't come back."

I had been in Dekalb county jail about a year, and when I first got there, I was all by himself. But on my way out I was taking Christ with me. At fifty-eight years of age I was walking out of jail with just the clothes on my back. Everything on the outside would be gone. Nothing I used to have would be waiting for me, my furniture, clothes, and photography equipment, my cars and bank accounts, and even my pictures, memorabilia and keepsakes, everything was gone.

I owned absolutely nothing.

I had no place to go and no way to get there, but with Jesus by my side, I would soon be standing in a world I thought I would never see again, the richest man alive.

36

The door opened and I stepped outside the cell block with a cold chill in my gut.

I had my sheets and thin wool blanket rolled up in my mattress. My extra jumpsuit was draped over one shoulder and I had a small sack with my toothbrush and toilet items and my pen and paper. I had everything I owned in my arms as I stepped out into the hallway.

I didn't have the feeling that I imagined an animal had, when taking him out of one cage, and placing him in another. You do that carefully so that he doesn't get away from you. But I didn't feel that this time. There were no chains, no handcuffs; no one seemed worried that I would get loose.

That was my first feel of being liberated.

The guard waiting for me simply said, "This way" and turned to a hallway and we walked side by side to a room where I turned in my bedding. Seconds later, I walked down another hallway to an elevator that took us to the basement, and into a room I entered a year ago.

It had a caged window that separated the waiting area from several rows of shelves with huge bins. A trustee walked up to the window with a box in his hands. On the top of the box a name and a number, written in black marker pen read, "TIRSCHEL 00498746". He handed me the box that held the clothes I was wearing a year ago, when I was arrested. They were dirty, ragged, and fit a little loose, but I felt like a real person again just wearing them. I pressed my hand against my chest to feel the soft silky shirt against me. I wondered how long this farce could possibly go on before someone, in this long drawn out process, catches the glitch in the paper work, and sends me back to "B" Pod.

Don't they understand?

I'm guilty, I admit it…I don't argue the point anymore. I didn't do what they say I did, but the crimes I did commit didn't make it to court.

I did take a life…my life…and I wasted it.

And in so doing, I tortured the four other lives in my family along with making miserable the lives of strangers I'll never know. I abandoned my children. I left my wife to care for them, Because, I was not man enough to do it myself. All because I was afraid that I could never do it, I didn't do it. So, since I was afraid to find out, I might not be the man I needed to be, I went in search of shortcuts and quick fix feelings that would hide the truth from me.

Those shortcuts took me away from home and away from my task at hand, and I went in search of serving my own self-seeking interests.

I was guilty.

I deserved to be right where I was, but someone was making a mistake and I was getting out. Less than an hour ago I was sitting behind bars looking at a minimum of twenty years to life and now, a mistake has been made, and I am being processed out.

How far will I get, by playing along with this error that they are making, and will I be in trouble for going along with it? I'm not to blame. It's not my job to tell them that I have no attorney, no court order; it's not my job to point out to them that there is no justification for any action to release me.

The ordeal of being processed out seemed to be taking forever.

The fear I lost inside my cell was creeping back into my life the closer I was getting to the outside world.

But I kept my mouth shut.

I didn't ask anybody anything for fear that they would look into the situation closer and see the mistake that was being made. I went from one window to another, and was now at the last window before going to the other side of the bars. At this window, a guard emptied a 9x12 brown manila envelope on the counter in front of me and I got my ring, watch, and my wallet.

The cash I had in my wallet, when I was processed in, wasn't there. It went on the "books", along with the money my daughter Cynthia put on my books every month. That was the money that made it possible for me to get my moon pies, hot fries, coffee, tea, and pads of paper and such.

There was still fifty dollars on the books that was coming to me, but I would have to wait and get a check cut from the accounting office.

All, in one second of time, and after the better part of an hour of being processed out, I passed through one last locked door and was out from behind any other locks or bars and I was standing in a large waiting room.

I could have walked out the door if I wanted to. I could be outside and I could walk down the street. I could go anywhere. It was so hard for me to grasp. It was like someone walked up to me and gave me a million dollars for no reason at all. It was beyond comprehension.

Instead of walking out, I looked across the room and saw the bright outdoors rush towards me through an unlocked open door. The warm orange sun was pouring through the door with the color of the green from the grass and that mixed brightly with the blue of a clear and open sky. Just outside the door next to the curb sat my daughter's red Saab convertible.

Tracy was there to pick me up.

When I saw her there I immediately realized I was never alone. Tracy made regular visits to me and even though I deserved nothing at all, my daughter Cynthia kept money on my books. That gave me the luxury that only someone inside who had moon pies, hot fries, and their own bag of coffee to negotiate trades and bargains would ever understand.

My son Derek held the family together the way I couldn't. He was the man that took over when I became the boy who got lost. He took care of his mother, his sisters, and was the role model for my grandson.

My kids may not have had the best father but their father sure had the best kids.

I was so excited, that I ran out the door and said, "Sweetheart, thank you…thank you. Hey listen, baby, I have to wait for a check, can you wait? If you can't we can go now."

Tracy smiled and said, "Slow down dad. It'll be alright."

"No, you don't understand, they're making a mistake. There's no reason for me to be getting out." I listened to myself and decided how terribly right I was, and changed my plan on the spot, "Come on, quick, lets get out of here."

It was right then, that I realized what a pitiful person I became.

I truly believed that they were making a mistake and that it would only be a matter of time before they would discover their mistake and lock me up again. I had no thought of getting away or of making a run for it. I just wanted to be out in the fresh air long enough to get a double steak burger, French fries, and a vanilla shake.

That was the level to which my life was reduced.

Any goal of success, or happiness, or being with anyone special, was replaced with the thought of having the freedom to eat junk food, just one more time in my life.

"No dad, relax. Go on back and get your money. You're going to need it."

She was right. I was going to need everything I could pull together. My two cars were gone and all my furniture, and my clothes and my photography equipment and everything I had been saving throughout my life...mementoes, old photos, and things that I never thought I would lose, it was all gone. I had nothing left of my life.

I didn't think I would ever need anything in my life again, beyond that one shot at a double cheeseburger and fries. But, I didn't want to look as scared, as the cowardly way I was feeling, so I said, "OK, baby...but I'm only going to wait a little bit" and I went back into the waiting area and took a seat.

I watched two sheriffs on the other side of the locked doors with papers in their hand. They were getting ready to walk out from where I had been processed and they were talking to one of the clerks behind the desk. The clerk pointed out to the waiting area and the two sheriffs looked in my direction and abruptly turned to come out the door. I jumped up and ran to the restroom and hid.

Opening the door just a crack, I watched the two officers walk out into the waiting area and approach another clerk on this side of the locked doors. They talked for a second, laughed, and then gave the clerk the papers and said, "Take care of that, we're going to lunch." They were talking about the Braves pitching staff as they walked out the door leading towards the parking lot.

I let the breath out I was holding and slowly came out of the rest room. I walked across the waiting area and sat down across from the window where the clerk would be calling my name.

I wiped the perspiration that was forming on my forehead and sat down to wait.

Twenty to thirty minutes had passed and the heat allowed my mind to drift into a fog as my eyelids grew heavy. An icy feeling got caught in a sudden gasp from my throat as the sound of my name over the PA system sat me up as straight as a board. "Tirschel, Window R."

I shot out of my seat and stood and waited for my head to clear before slowly walking over to the clerk sitting behind a glass window under a sign that said, "Window R". She gave me a check for the money that was mine, and I thanked her and started for the door.

It was killing me to walk so slowly. I wanted to run but I was afraid to look too much in a hurry. I nearly suffocated in that walk to my daughter's car. But, when I got in the passenger's side, I sat down and let out a deep breath, "Thanks baby, let's go."

My children talked their mother into letting me live in her basement and she agreed to give me one meal a day if I fixed things around the house, with the agreement, that when I could afford it, I would pay her $100 a week.

The room was nice. I was able to watch TV in the basement den and I had my own bathroom. I bought this house quite a few years ago when we were still together and she did a fine job at keeping it up when I left. I was comfortable there and wanted to stay as long as I could but my better judgment told me to get out of Georgia and make a run for it before the mistake was found and they came to get me.

It was a comfort, having nothing at all.

As long as I had a place to sleep and food to eat, I was a satisfied. I knew I would get caught if I stayed, but I didn't want to leave. Just the same though, and just out of instinct, I ran and hid in the back yard whenever I heard a car slow down in front of the house. I thought surely it would be but a matter of time before the Sheriff's Department would discover their mistake, and so I spent a great deal of time hiding in the back yard.

Some days, I walked down the railroad tracks, through the small city of Forest Park, just to stay away from the house. I wanted to enjoy this mistake the Department of Corrections made for as long as I could before I went back in. I was getting too old to go on the run again.

Each day I just enjoyed the fresh air and the sunshine, and I sat peacefully on the railroad tracks, or in the park. I just sat anywhere that I felt safe, and outside of the long arm of the law, just until it got dark. Then I went back to the house and listened to the cars driving by outside.

A couple weeks went by, and since no sheriffs were knocking on the door, I called an attorney friend, "Hey Annie, it's the Duke."

"Well, well, you aren't calling collect. So, I guess 'somebody up there likes you'.

I remembered Annie was a boxing buff, "That's something Rocky Graziano would say."

She laughed, "You still got it, baby. So, what's the story? How did you get out?"

"That's what I was wondering."

"Damn Duke, now what did you do?"

"No, I'm clean…they just let me out. Don't know why. That's why I'm calling you."

"You mean Dekalb County just…just let you go. Just like that."

"Yeah, really…I think they made a mistake."

"When was it?" She sounded curious.

"Two weeks ago."

"Didn't anyone say why…did you ask?"

I tried to explain, "No way. I figured they were making a mistake and I wasn't going to point it out to them. But now, I might as well be on the run…I look over my shoulder, and I stay away from the house. And I need to get a job, or something…I need to get into something, but I keep thinking I'll be going back in, any day…as soon as they realize what happened."

There was silence on the other end.

I asked cautiously, "Is there some way you…I mean, could you ask…you know, in a way that won't bring it to anyone's attention. I just want to know. One way or the other, I want to make a decision and…and, I'm just not sure what's happening."

"No problem, I'll make a couple calls. Where you going to be later today?"

"I'm not sure. What time?"

"Oh, about three. I should know something by then. I have to be in court this morning, shouldn't take me long. Give me a call about three this afternoon."

I felt a huge weight was lifted from me.

This was a perfect day to walk down the railroad tracks, and so I stopped by the little store on the corner, and bought six cold cans of Squirt soda pop. I finished one of the sodas before I crossed the street, and climbed the rocks on the embankment leading up to the tracks. I followed the tracks away from town, and stopped about a mile or so away from everything.

The sun was bright, the sky was blue, and a few puffy white clouds were floating so low, I could see every fold in them. I sat on a rock on one side of the trestle and thought about absolutely nothing. I just enjoyed the day. I never enjoyed my days the way I did now. Now, that I wasn't locked up in a cage. Although, I didn't have any place to go, I felt so free to know, I *could* go, if I wanted.

I just sat on that rock, enjoying my thoughts of being free, and drinking my soda. I sat there until late afternoon, and I may have dozed off a time or two, but no trains came by all day. The air held a stillness that cushioned any sound from getting to me, except that occasional honking of a horn, off in the distance, that made me feel how far away I was from the world.

The sun was going down, and my sodas were gone when I remembered, I had a telephone call to make. Reluctantly, I rose and dusted my pants off, and began the walk back into my world.

I went to the pay phone at the little market and called my attorney friend.

Annie had great news.

She discovered that Damon dropped the armed robbery charges on me, and moved away, a long time ago. And the armed robbery charge, that the judge was so anxious to see me face, was shelved by way of a "non-pros".

"A what?"

Annie said, "A "non-pros"…for "non-prosecute". When the office of the District Attorney has an over load of cases they go through each case and judge the merits of each case, separately. The DA's office will set aside a case, or a number of cases, in a classification known as a "Non-Pros"; which means they stop the prosecution, pending the introduction of any further evidence, or activity. Any activity that comes up relative to the case can cause the reopening of the file, and it would go back on the docket, and the person they released would be re-arrested."

"You mean…I'm really free?"

"Exactly…you're good to go."

After we hung up, I sat on the curb and took it all in.

Finally, something was making sense.

The people accusing me of putting a gun to Billy's head, and stealing his car, were known drug dealers. Billy, himself, was just released from a 17 year prison term for shooting a police helicopter out of the air.

On my side of the ledger, I was the best, and most well known, Defensive Tactics instructor at the Georgia Police Academy. It could be possible that the differences between my accusers and me could have swung things my way.

It might even have something to do with the fact that I didn't do what they said I did.

I wasn't guilty of the charges they had on me, but I wasn't living a life that was innocent either. I was innocent of the charges of armed robbery, but I was guilty of a dozen other crimes.

It seemed to even out, it didn't matter what name you wanted to call it.

The greatest crime I committed though wasn't against the state.

It was against God.

God had a plan for my life and I did everything imaginable to wreck His plan by wrecking my life.

I believe, with all my heart that being released from prison was not a factor of anything important in my life. Being released from prison was a minor point, when compared to what I was released from, after I accepted my relationship with Jesus Christ.

It was my new relationship with Christ that set me free, but it just wasn't in God's plan to keep me locked behind bars. I was released from prison because of the relationship I accepted with Jesus Christ, but my relationship wasn't dependant on my being released. I would have gladly stayed in, if that was where the Lord wanted to use me.

The Lord has something for me to do, and I believe I need to be on the outside to do it. I was released so that I can do what God has for me to do.

37

When I learned of the "Non-Pros", I realized my release wasn't an oversight after all, and I was able to stop looking over my shoulder.

There was a reason why I went through what I went through, and it wasn't just about me.

I was "dead" in the water.

At fifty-eight years old I was behind bars for a year, looking at twenty years to life, with no chance of me seeing day light again. But God wanted me to be back in the world for a reason. It wasn't to run off and lick my wounds and say, "Oh boy; that was a close one" and then hide.

But neither was I to go back into the type of world that buried me.

There is something specific God wanted from me.

To know what God wanted me to do was going to take more than *"leaning into my own understanding."* I wasn't going to just *know* automatically what God wanted from me. I was going to need to search for it and *find* what it was he wanted me to do.

God plan was not just to get me released from prison and then float around. I figured He wanted me to get back into the world. But, as soon as I got back into the world; I felt the world starting to get back into me.

I came to the conclusion to start normalizing my life by getting back into a routine with which I was familiar. I felt most comfortable when I was working out, and so I made the decision to walk over to a Forest Park gym, known as Muscle World, with a proposition: I offered to teach karate for them if I could work-out in their weight room. If they didn't want the karate, I was going to ask if I could join their gym, and pay for it when I got a job.

The owner, Bobby Jordan, was at the front desk when I walked in. Bobby's a huge man. I think someone said he was a Mr. America at one time, I know he should be. He's the kind of guy that when he walks towards you, you step aside. You move out of his way because, if for no other reason, his mass takes up all the space around you, and you have to move, or just get crushed.

I knew of Bobby when I lived in Forest Park but I never met him.

He talked in a slow soft spoken southern accent, "You used to have that place down on Ash Street, didn't you? I heard of you, but…listen, about the karate lessons, I don't think so. Nah, we're doing construction in this room over here and we really don't have the room for karate right now."

"When will the room be finished?"

"It'll be awhile yet."

"I'm not working yet, but, you know. What are the payments here anyway?"

"So, you don't have a job?"

"Yeah, I've been away awhile."

"Go ahead and work out, you can pay me when you get work. We'll work it out somehow. Go on…grab a work out now if you want."

"No thanks, I just wanted to check it out. I have to look at a house that needs some cleanup work done on it."

"Ok, but when you're ready, come on back."

"Thanks man, I really appreciate it." I turned and started out the door.

I was half way out the door when Bobby called out, "Hey, by the way, what are doing Monday night?"

"Monday night?" His question puzzled me and I paused as I thought about it. I wondered what could be going on so special on Monday night.

"Yeah, Monday; 7pm."

"Nothing…I guess. Why?"

"Come on by Monday night, we have bible study here. You're welcome."

At Muscle World, who would have known? I shrugged, "Yeah…Ok."

There was Bobby, Greg, Jerry and the Pastor R.C. Banks, and all the other muscle heads that met every Monday night and talked about their love for the Lord. The bible study was scheduled each Monday night from 7pm to 8pm but was rarely over until 9:30 or 10.

What a sight it was, all these strong and powerful people, admitting how weak they were without the Lord. Sometimes, one of us would need attention to a specific issue in our life and the others would discuss what would best fit the situation according to scripture and common sense.

In some of the first meetings I was being guided around a particular decision facing me.

I took a job at a friend's nightclub because he wanted me to stop the gangs from wrecking his club. It was simple enough. We used metal detectors and wouldn't allow any guns in the club. We gained the respect of the gang members because we didn't turn them in, we just turned them away. They would go away quietly, and in a few minutes they would be back, without their gun.

Then we banned any group from wearing their 'colors" inside. They could stay but they would have to take off their "colors". In a matter of weeks the hostilities were under control.

Unfortunately, the owner of the club chose to make it the "home" for some major drug people by catering to a few major drug figures while banning anyone who would cause trouble for them. The local thug and his boys could function as they wished without worrying about the law or their own personal competition.

I became faced with one of those choices I used to have to make and I immediately fell back into my old pattern of thinking. I told myself that I may have been "in the water" but I was not "of the water". I convinced myself that I was just in a boat in the water, and since I was not actually *in* the water, I wouldn't be affected by the water. In other words, I convinced myself that because of my relationship with God I could be around those people and not be affected by what they were doing around me.

I tried to believe that I was strong enough to walk in the midst of that crowd and not be touched by what once put me away. It wasn't their drugs that controlled my thinking, it was being thought of as the "man".

I felt like a big "man" when I was asked to force people to pay their debt.

I felt like quite the "man" when I escorted the prostitutes on their "outcalls" or watched over a group of "working" girls getting down at a bachelor party. It was that activity that made me feel like a "man" and it was that activity that pulled me out of the boat and into the water.

It was that type of thinking that would guarantee that sooner or later, some dealer would want me to do them a favor and my ego would get the best of me, and I would not only get wet, I would drown.

It was in one these extended bible studies at Muscle World that I was led to a scripture that said, "Once you place your hand on the plow and look back, you are not fit for the kingdom of God." It was out of those meetings with the Muscle World bible study, and the concern those muscle heads had for me, that a light was thrown on my situation.

It took a couple of weeks to sink in, but I knew they were right to warn me against keeping my job at the club, but I didn't have another job to go to. So, for awhile I was working it just for the money, but then came the day that I felt that feeling I once had. I remembered how much I enjoyed being around that low life crowd I used to know.

That thought alone woke me to the reality that I was slipping.

38

I held on to a dozen reasons why I wouldn't slip this time, but I kept running into the old crowd, and I started feeling at home in this crowd that I thought was no longer me. I also turned a blind eye to the dope deals going down, and when I did, I got *that* feeling, that all too welcome feeling, that used to come over me, when I was offered a 'line' of speed.

I turned it down this time; but what about the next?

It bothered me to know how hard it was for me to pass it up, and I was surprised that I secretly hoped it would be offered again.

To tell you the truth, I didn't want to turn it down.

With all my commitment to Christ, I still did not *want* to turn down that line of speed, but I did. But, it was still becoming very clear to me, how easy it could be for me to be pulled away from God. I was reminded of how easy the demons come back to an empty house once it's been cleaned out.

Immediately, I felt as empty as I ever felt when I was living on the street.

That scared me, because I wanted to fill that feeling of emptiness up, or else chase it away. I felt certain I would have done one or the other with whatever was offered to me next.

So, I ducked out and went home early.

That night scared me.

If I decide to start living my life on purpose, I better make a decision how serious I really am about living it right. It was time to quit thinking, that just because I accepted Jesus in my life, I could put my life on auto pilot, and I'd always be able to glide right out of every filthy thing I flew into.

Believing in God does not give me God's power.

God's power is God's power, not mine.

Before I can access God's power in my life I'm going to have to accept and follow a set of conditions that start with turning to God and asking for help and then, do what it is He tells me.

Since I couldn't sleep anyway I got up as soon as the sun did and I waited in my room until the sun melted the dew off the leaves in the back yard. When the sun warmed away the morning chill I went outside and climbed to the highest point that was the furthest away from the house and sat beneath a huge old tree. That was the spot where I used to hide each time I heard a car go by when I thought my release was accidental.

I decided to look for something that will tell me directly why I shouldn't keep my job, or else, find some justification for thinking I can keep the job without getting burnt.

And lately, I had been able to pray on an issue and then open the bible and find what I needed to know on the exact page that I opened. I saw it as God's way of helping me because I was so unknowledgeable when it came to scripture. This particular morning I decided to get off to myself at the high point in the back yard, and see if I could leave the decision I had to make, to this "biblical toss of the coin".

I opened the bible at random and my eyes fell down on to the page in front of me and the first thing my eyes focused on was Proverbs 4:14-15, *"Enter not on the path of the wicked, and go not in the way of evil men. Avoid it, pass not by it, turn from it, and pass away."*

I laughed and got up from where I sat and ran inside the house. I couldn't wait to tell Pastor Banks of how the decision was chosen to quit that job but it was too early to call anyone. I was amazed that this way of asking God for help worked so precisely the way it worked for me again, today. I wanted to tell somebody what happened but I couldn't get a hold of anyone and so I decided to just enjoy this miracle for myself and do what it told me to do. Later in the day I went down to the club and gathered up whatever belongings I had there, and then followed the instructions: *"I turned from it."*

My life was born again in prison, but I was just starting to live again right then. That was my starting-over point for my life. I was given a choice and I chose the right one, but I didn't do it on my own. Several months before that day, I asked God to let me make my own choices again and he did. He let me make my own choices, because I chose Him first, and then I took action on the decision He wanted me to make. He wanted me to discover for myself that I would never be strong enough to make decisions without Him.

It was a start, a real good start.

Shortly after I quit the job at Joe's Place, I chose a course that put me on a closer walk with God. I entered The Jacksonville Theological Seminary and Pastor Banks was kind enough to let me do my intern work as his associate pastor at the All Saints Church of God. And then I went through Chuck Colson's Prison Ministry and discipleship training and I ended up joining the Hope Prison Ministry at Charles Stanley's 1st Baptist Church in Atlanta.

When I used to run the streets, I lost a lot of my friends to either death, or drugs, and now I'm not running the streets any longer, but I'm losing a lot of other friends to decision.

Some of my friends from the street can't find their way out of the struggle they're in and they're getting lost, but I still get around to the old haunts and try to reach who I can. Those friends who accepted Christ, when I was lost, didn't forget me either, because when I showed up for my walk with the Lord, they were there waiting for me.

One Monday night I was getting ready to leave my room to go to bible study and the phone rang. I picked it up and recognized the voice immediately, "Duke Tirschel…Chuck Norris."

Chuck had been my friend for thirty years.

But one day, I fell off the end of the earth and we lost touch. I separated myself from my friends, from my family, and from God. As soon as I heard his voice I laughed, and my first words to him after five years of no contact were, "Why you ol' turkey you…how you been?"

"Working harder than ever. How you doing?"

"Oh…you know. I'm doing Ok. I was just getting ready to…"

He sounded excited when he interrupted me, "Bob Wall gave me a letter you wrote him a while back."

"When was that?"

"Couple weeks ago. I don't know. He's been keeping me up to date. I know you had some problems, but from what Bob tells me, you've made quite a few changes in your life."

Chuck had been to all parts of this world, and had seen things I didn't even know existed. Among his personal friends are the most glamorous and successful people, and the most influential dignitaries anyone could have. Yet, when he heard I got up from where I had fallen in life, he took the time to call and to let me know he cared. It was Chuck who encouraged me to keep standing.

He did that by telling me exactly where he stood.

As I listened to him, I got the impression that he was on a mission. I got the feeling that, after five years going by, he had a better reason for calling me than to just say hi. It was as though God tapped him on the shoulder and said, "I need you now…we can use this guy. It's time to call him."

Chuck had accomplished so much in his life before that night that he called me, but there was only one thing he was most proud of, and that was to tell me that he was a Christian.

He called again the following night, and this time he told me of the Christian influence his wife Gena had on his life. A month later I flew to LA from Atlanta to workout with him and he shared his testimony with me. It was then, that I felt the strength he was giving me. The sharing of his testimony confirmed and strengthened my walk with Jesus.

I needed that type of support from my Christian friends, once I hit the street again. In prison, we all had that "jail-house" religion, and we said our "fox-hole" prayers, but the hardest life to live isn't living behind bars, it's being out, in the world of free choice.

When I got out I was faced with decisions, and there were those short-cuts staring me in the face again. I needed to hear other men speak up and confess their faith.

The questions as to whether I was man enough to succeed came up again, too. Could I compete with other men for a good job, a decent living, or a loving relationship? It used to be easier for me to verbally, or physically attack whatever scared me. It used to be too hard for me to face what was challenging me, because then I'd have to become the man I was afraid to be, and so, I struck out in any way I felt safe.

But, God was going to let me make my own choices again. It seems the enemy doesn't come after you as hard as he does, until you have a choice to make. And he even hits you harder when he thinks you'll choose Jesus. But when you do choose Jesus, and when He walks into your life, the devil has to go.

In prison I begged God to trust me again. I was so sure that I would be able to be trusted, but now, I see that it was only because I didn't have the access to all those wrong choices. Being back out in the world makes it so easy to make the wrong choices, because they stand right there next to the correct ones. It wasn't long before the very trust I begged God to give me was being tested again

But, I had friends.

And just like making a muscle stronger, my walk with Christ grew stronger. First my walk grew stronger with support and guidance from others whom I respected, then by attending the bible studies at Muscle World, and ultimately by my own personal pursuit of a closer relationship with God.

I had to do what God told me to do. And God did with me, in the *spiritual,* as He did with Israel, in the *physical.* He said to cross the "Jordan" and take the "promised" land.

My "Jordan" was the fear of not being "good" enough at anything.

For forty years I have been searching for the "promised land" and when I got there I saw *giants* among men, they were well-educated, they dressed well, and drove nice cars, they were gifted in a business sense, and they seemed far superior to me in so many ways, and they had money and that really scared me.

I thought I couldn't survive.

The "giants" scared me into thinking that whatever I tried to achieve I would fall short and I didn't want anyone to find out that someone might be better than me.

In the boxing ring, I stayed just long enough to win every match I fought, but I quickly retired from competition before anyone could beat me. In karate competition, I won a few major tournaments and then stopped competing. I was afraid I wouldn't have been able to take the loss. I worked hard and did well in my career pursuits but I changed jobs whenever I approached the responsibility of success.

And so, like the Israelites, instead of crossing "my Jordan" and competing for the riches of God's inheritance, I stayed in the wilderness and fought for nothing,

I fought for forty years and struggled through college, survived one job after another, sabotaged relationships and sunk so many opportunities where I could have received what God had planned for me.

God's first commandment was "to be fruitful" and to use His gifts to do what He created me to do. But, I spent too much time fighting life to discover why I was created or what I was to do, and subsequently, I did nothing.

God told Israel to cross the Jordan too, and they didn't do it.

They stayed in the wilderness for the same reason I did, they were afraid. They saw giants and they were afraid. They thought they would lose if they went up against the Giants and so they did what I did. They stayed in the wilderness and fought against God.

The Israelites wandered forty years in the wilderness, and so did I.

They fought for every step they took, and so did I.

But when the battles were over, neither of us owned a thing, not even the step we just fought for. We were protected by God, but we had nothing to show for our battles, because we wouldn't do what God told us to do.

I was stuck in no-man's land.

I was lost in plain sight.

I existed, but I didn't live.

I fought to make a living but I failed to earn a life. All I ever earned was exactly what the Israelites earned; the right to fight for another day.

Listen; even when we cross the Jordan as God told us to do, we still have to fight, but now, every where we set our foot belongs to us, because we fought the battle, but Jesus won the war.

And when I accepted Christ, I *died to self* and I did what God had told me to do. Only then, did I too, begin to gain a foothold on life.

Your "Jordan" is whatever scares you from doing what God has told you to do. Your "Jordan" is whatever scares you from finding God's purpose for your life. Get over it…cross your "Jordan".

I passed through that open prison door and crossed my Jordan when I accepted the relationship Jesus wanted to have with me. I still face Giants, but now I beat them. I have victory through Christ who strengthens me and He promised me that no weapon formed against me will prosper.

God said to me, "Ok, now let's get to work."

First I fixed, cleaned, and painted some old houses for a friend of mine and he gave me an old car worth $150 for my work. Then I rented some camera equipment and photographed a karate school. I did that a few more times until I could buy some used equipment and a better car.

I traveled to Kansas City on my way to California and preached to 100 boys in McCune Boys Home in Independence Missouri. It was the Boys Home I was sent to over forty years ago. I had a message that I wanted to bring to the boys there, and that message was, *"It Doesn't Have To Be This Way,* and some of those boys *heard* me.

Three years ago, I reached California where I faced more "giants". There was unemployment, transportation problems, and for several months I slept on the street. There was illness, depression, and hunger. There were strained relationships, broken ones and loneliness.

Those were the giants I faced, and fought, and because I took no short-cuts and gave no quarter, God always gave me the ground on which I stood. My God is an awesome God, my God is an on-time God. I still had to show up for the game. I still had to stand up to the plate. And I still had to learn to be everything God created me to be; and do you know what? I like what He created me to be…for the first time in my life; I like me.

I found out that my major goal wasn't to get out of prison.

My major goal was to find peace, and I found it.

I found it at the foot of the cross.

Jesus was waiting for me there, and when he saw me coming, He couldn't wait to tell me…*that in His Father's house there were many man-*

sions. I felt His peace as He gently touched my hand, and with the kindest smile I ever knew, He said, *"I go to prepare a place for you."* I wanted to remind Him about that day in my cell when I accepted the relationship He wanted to have with me, and so I said, "Before you go, make a home in my heart."

And He did.

I ask you, could someone search your heart and find Christ living there? If you were accused of being a Christian could anyone look at your life and find enough evidence to convict you?

As for me and my house... *"We stand convicted."*

Conclusion

In a message given by T.D. Jakes, the bishop yelled, "Is there a man in the house?" And every male who was there, stood up. Wouldn't every male alive want to be able to be honest in answering that call? What a terrible thing it would be, if one lone, grown male sat, unable to rise to answer the call, and be acknowledged as a man.

A time will come for every boy, when he will be called upon, to go through the process of growing from adolescence into manhood.

The process doesn't just "happen" after a certain number of years. It will happen by the boy himself, as he goes through the conditions to which he must rise. In him are the genes that he must quicken, and it is the boy himself who chooses to become the man. He is an active participant, not just the recipient of something happening to him.

Our society has organizations, clubs, and activities, in which boys participate with certain rituals, so that they can find the tools to affect this transformation into manhood.

Single mothers bring their young boys to karate classes, boxing lessons, and encourage their sons to spread their wings by playing football, going to camp, and being active in the Boy Scouts.

Fathers too, try to point their sons towards the sports, colleges, and the family business, and along the paths that helped them become who they are.

The majority of boys growing up today don't have someone reliable to point them in the right direction. These boys are just like all those other boys who did have the proper encouragement, the solid motivation, and the intelligent and gifted guidance. They want to become a man too, just as much as the boys who are exposed to careful nurturing.

God even tells us that we are to become a man.

In Ephesians 1:18, Paul said, "That God may give unto you the spirit of wisdom and revelation in the knowledge of him; that the eyes of your understanding being enlightened; that ye may know what is the hope of his calling."

Unfortunately, too many of us took off from that point and went through trial and error in search of what our lives should be, and in most cases, we went with what felt good, rather than what *was* good. But, in a rough and painful process, many boys did make it to that place we call manhood.

When I accepted my relationship with Jesus Christ in prison, I was contented to stay there. A scripture in Isaiah said, "He who walks in righteousness…such a man will dwell on the heights; his place of defense will be the fortress of rocks; his bread will be given him, water for him will be for sure."

I had that in prison, and that was all I needed in life.

But, God's plan for my life, meant *life* needed more from me.

Some of us go for quite some time before we feel as though we have really connected with being "all the man that we can be". It's not uncommon to face certain conditions that raise questions about are ability to *make it* in the world.

All too often though, we respond to those questions that challenge us, by grabbing worthless labels, in an effort to prove that we're a "man".

Face it, we all feel weak sometimes. And, when we feel weak, it's because we are just human and it's alright. That's what God made us to be. Find comfort in knowing that God promised us that, "No weapon formed against us will prosper."

For anyone who wants to "be all the man that he can be", or simply wants to be the man God created him to be, I can testify to the fact that you *can* get there from here.

Just, trust God, and turn your attention towards the cross, look at the life of Jesus; and then, look at the life Jesus has waiting for you.

About the Author

R.L. "Duke" Tirschel, co-authored two books on fitness and martial arts with his instructor of 35 years, Chuck Norris, and presently heads a Christian Karate Ministry.

978-0-595-67129-8
0-595-67129-2

Printed in the United States
28585LVS00001B/190-201

9 780595 671298